Praise

'An inspiring book about leading your finest life.'
— **Robin Sharma**, #1 worldwide bestselling
author of *The 5am Club* and *The Monk Who
Sold His Ferrari*

'Everything it takes to become a champion, Calvin
has covered in *WILD Success*. I highly suggest this
book because it is definitely a good read.'
— **Ronnie Coleman**, 8 times Mr Olympia
and a body building icon

'This is a timely and essential book for our
challenging world. Calvin is a true master and
deeply inspiring. *WILD Success* will help you
improve your life, achieve more, and expand your
consciousness.'
— **Jack Delosa**, $100m+ entrepreneur and
investor, 2 times best-selling author and
5 times AFR Young Rich List member

'After a decade traveling the world changing lives,
Calvin has distilled his best lessons in psychology,
coaching, peak performance and therapy into this
practical, hands-on-guide. A must-read for anyone
looking to improve their WILD life – Wellness,
Income, Love and Direction.'
— **Daniel Priestley**, author of *Entrepreneur
Revolution* and founder of Dent Global

'Calvin has a unique ability to talk directly to you with every word that is written. If you want to truly achieve more in one year than most do in a decade, read *WILD Success*.'
— **Ryan Tuckwood**, Network 10's SHARK TANK 2018 and founder of SWISH Sales Coaching

'*WILD Success* is the perfect guide for anyone who wants to succeed in every area of their life! I wish I read this book as an 18-year-old. Great work, Calvin.'
— **Glenn 'The 6 Million Dollar Man' Austin**, 3 times WA State Boxing Champion

'*WILD Success* should be on the book list in every school in the country; just imagine a world where our children know how to take control of their emotions, beliefs and behaviours. What a world that would be.'
— **Simon Rawadi**, AFR Fast 100 co-founder of Sly Group of Companies

'*WILD Success* is a well-written, insightful and practical guide to creating the life of your dreams. Calvin's approach is both inspiring and actionable, and the book is filled with valuable advice, exercises and real-life examples that will help you achieve your goals and live a fulfilling life. I would highly recommend this book to anyone who wants to take control of their life and create the future they desire.'
— **Rhonda Swan**, CEO of Unstoppable Branding Agency and author of international best-selling *Women Gone Wild* Series

'Calvin weaves together psychology, personal mastery and spirituality in a uniquely practical way to help anyone take control of their lives. His writing style is no-nonsense, clear, personal, easy-to-read, and even exciting. His book is a must-read, not only for coaches and consultants but also for virtually anyone who wants to improve their lives!'

> — **Tim Guest**, Managing Director of Infinite Wealth, 40 Under 40, and Entrepreneur of the Year (2015)

'Inspiring, thought-provoking and transformational. *WILD Success* will help you create a road map to wealth, health and happiness. A must-read!'

> — **Neil Gibb**, founder and Managing Director of The HMO Property Co and JNG Property Group

'A Wild Life is the only life you should be living, and Calvin has encapsulated the essence of what it is to live that life to the fullest. Essential reading for anyone wanting more.'

> — **Brett and Marie Jones**, founders of The Relationship Code

'Anyone who wants to develop the mindset to succeed needs to read *WILD Success*.'

> — **Mark Ottobre**, founder of Enterprise Fitness Australia

CALVIN COYLES

WILD SUCCESS

Breakthrough Your Limitations and
Live the Life of Your Dreams

R^ethink

First published in Great Britain in 2023
by Rethink Press (www.rethinkpress.com)

To Ron and Bernadette who risked it all so that I could live a WILD life. Without you, none of this would be possible.

Contents

Introduction

We are living in the greatest moment in human history. No, I haven't gone mad, and yes, I'm aware that I'm writing these words in the aftermath of the greatest social disruption since the Second World War – the COVID-19 pandemic. Yet, I stand behind my statement. It's the best time to be alive for people like you and me: people who are prepared to accept absolute responsibility for their lives. People eager to pursue the road less travelled and to seek out what I call the 'Wild Path'.

The global pandemic has flipped the switch on 'the great reset', which is seeing people quit their jobs en masse, with no replacement or plan. They just know they aren't willing to settle for a life void of fulfilment. The work-from-home orders gave millions of people a taste of a different reality, one that had been reserved for the ultra-wealthy, and now they won't settle for anything less. To those people we say, 'Welcome to the WILD.' The pandemic has impacted our lives in different ways; whatever your experience has been, this is your opportunity to do your own reset and create the life of your dreams.

This book brings together my best work, skills, tools and strategies in the field of human potential, compiled from my experience of working with more than 200,000 clients from nearly a hundred countries. It is a manual for deep transformation, self-discovery and human growth. My goal is to be practical, pragmatic and direct; to give you everything you need and nothing you don't. I'll let you decide if I have succeeded. This book serves as a guide, a treasure map, a precious resource for anyone wanting to transform their life. More importantly, it's for anyone ready to learn how to help others do the same. I hope this book will become an oft-used resource on your journey toward a life of fulfilment and purpose, what I refer to as 'living a WILD life'.

The cornerstone of the book is a three-step process cultivated through my combined experiences – I call it the WILD Method™. In the pages to come, I'll help you cultivate a *compelling vision* for your future, so clear you can see it and taste it. Then, in learning about *internal alignment* we'll methodically work through any internal blocks and barriers that are preventing you from reaching your dreams. Finally, we'll craft a *proven strategy* that will help you achieve more in the next year than most achieve in a decade.

In our closing chapter, you'll discover the 7 Steps to WILD Success, which will serve as your roadmap for success, fulfilment and the accomplishment of your wildest dreams. Ahead of this journey, I must warn you: be careful what you ask for, because you might just get it.

I wrote this book for you, the men and women taking the road less travelled – the dreamers, rebels and wild ones who refuse to take no for an answer. The everyday heroes and hustlers who are trying to make themselves and everyone they come into contact with better. I have faith that this book will serve you in a profound way. I am also writing for my daughter, Alila Rae Coyles. I hope, like you, she finds wisdom, truth and guidance in these pages, and that she's proud of the work her dad does to make, in his own small way, the world a better place.

Here's to your success. Let's begin our journey into the WILD.

PART ONE
A LIFE OF CAPTIVITY

1
A Fundamental Choice

In the following chapters, you'll find a series of ideas, tools and strategies that have the power to transform your mindset, relationships, finances and career. You'll discover how to shift limiting beliefs, master your emotions, rewire your brain for success and defeat self-sabotage along the way. But the wisdom and resources contained within these pages are useless unless you embrace one fundamental choice: to live what I refer to as a 'WILD life', rather than a life of captivity.

You choose a WILD life by committing yourself to live life on your own terms. You choose a life of freedom and personal empowerment. You choose a life of absolute responsibility and extreme ownership over your past, present and future. You reject a life where you are captive to others' expectations. You reject a life of apathy and conformity. You assume responsibility for your life's direction. Consciously making this choice is the first step on any journey to success and fulfilment. Without it, you will always be a captive, living a shadow of the life of your dreams and never experiencing what life truly has to offer.

People who experience hardship often wish for an easy (or at least easier) life, but the antidote to suffering and hardship isn't a life of ease – it's a life of purpose. I want a life full of meaningful challenges, a life where the absolute best of me is called upon daily to step up and serve at the highest levels. A life well lived, with impact resulting in a lasting legacy. I dare say, if you're reading this book, that you also desire a WILD life. A life where the challenges are of your own making, tackled head on, in your own way and on your own terms. As actor Denzel Washington once said, 'Ease is a greater threat to progress than hardship.'[1]

The surest way to live a life of ease is to settle – to let go of your ambitions, lower your standards and accept that this is as good as it gets. Snuggle deep into that comfort zone. Sure, you'll feel a sense of relief in the moment but, over time, a dark cloud of disappointment and resentment will hover over your life, stealing that initial peace. In the wild, the cycle of life is black and white: you are either growing or you're dying; your soul is either expanding or it's contracting.

---

1   Erik McKay, 'Denzel Washington NAACP Image Awards 2017 Speech [FULL VIDEO]' (2017), www.youtube.com/watch?v=ZFPmyCTlxQw, accessed 30 May 2023

I can't make the choice for you; you have to decide what you want from life. You have to make the fundamental choice to take control of your destiny and live life on your terms. Now, a fair warning – there are no guarantees of success. I cannot promise that you will succeed and that it will be glorious. It's likely that you will fail and it will be devastating. What I know about you though, without having ever met you, is that you'll get back up and go again, because you're not a quitter. You're someone who plays to win and loves a challenge – it is in those qualities that you will find your success.

Remember, a ship that never leaves the harbour won't be smashed by the winds of change – but that is not what a ship is built for.

A life of captivity

In 2010, I was invited by an Australian charity to travel to Africa to establish a micro-financing project for women of the Korogocho slum in Nairobi, Kenya. The trip was a life-changing experience in many ways. I was instantly hit by a culture shock. I come from a working class background, which I had considered to be below average in regard to living standards. Yet by comparison with what I saw in Korogocho, it seemed the height of luxury.

The Korogocho slum is one of the largest in Africa, with between 150,000 and 200,000 people living within 1.5 square kilometres. The name Korogocho means 'crowded shoulder to shoulder' in Swahili. The slum is a collection of shanty huts erected using scrap metals from the nearby rubbish tip. There is no infrastructure, no clean water, no sanitation and the minimal of government support.

The first thing you notice when you arrive in Korogocho is the smell. The living conditions and proximity to waste produce a mix of odours putrid enough to make your eyes water. What was equally as shocking as the smell and the in-your-face poverty is the genuine happiness of the men, women and children of the community. I found them unbelievably joyous. At first, I thought this was an act for our benefit but, after twenty-four hours in Korogocho, I realised how happy the residents are and how simple their life is.

My brief for the trip was simple: to work with a group of women in the slums to help them establish business ventures that could support the community and become long-term sources of income. Easy? Not quite. No one told me that the women I would be working with spoke little to no English and that a Swahili translator was required to communicate with them. Also, the highest level of education among the group of sixteen women was equivalent to four years of primary school. A further complication was that, in most cases, the women had never been responsible for money (culturally, this was a role for the man of the household). Unfortunately, these women had been widowed and had no way to provide for their families.

How do you teach business, money management and wealth creation to a group of people who haven't completed primary school and can't speak English? You teach them how to play Monopoly. I can confirm that, universally, people fight, argue and go to any lengths to bankrupt each other when playing that game. After that, the first activity I asked the women to complete was a 'dream life' exercise. I cover this later in the book but, simply put, you create a vision board of what you would love to have in your life, if money weren't an issue. As I worked through this with each of the women, four ideas came up again and again. There were no fancy cars, private islands, yachts or expensive designer bags. The Korogocho women wanted four fundamental things: to send their kids to school, to run their own business, to be able to buy their own home and to have their own toilet with fresh, clean water. None of these is revolutionary and the cost of acquiring these essentials, taken for granted in large parts of the world, worked out at just AU\$4.70 per day. For less than the price of a cup of coffee in Perth, Western Australia, these women could have their dream life in Nairobi. This outcome was humbling.

I worked with the women of the community to establish the Mumma Shujaa (meaning Warrior Woman) programme. Together we created three businesses – a café, a taxi service and a hairdressing salon – all run by the women, for the women and their children. Each business was an incredible success and changed the lives of countless members of the Korogocho community.

Toward the end of our trip, I took a day away from the classroom to visit the Masai Mara National Reserve. This was my first experience of a natural reserve, a place where animals are protected yet free to roam in their natural habitat, living in harmony with nature and humans alike. I'll never forget seeing Africa's 'Big Five': the lion, leopard, rhino, elephant and African buffalo. A lioness and her cubs were curious enough to come to within five metres of our safari jeep, which made for an incredible experience.

On the five-hour drive home, I sat looking out the window and thinking about the paradox of my time in Africa. I had witnessed people with nothing display profound happiness. For the first time, I understood the meaning of community and how suffering brings people together. I had also been privileged to see Africa's Big Five in their natural habitat, an experience that had been indescribable and completely unlike a flashy Australian zoo, where animals are kept behind fences or in glass-walled enclosures for the enjoyment of visitors between 9am and 5pm.

Without this first-hand experience, I knew that my family and friends would fail to grasp the nuance of how it could be that the Korogocho women, who have so little, are wealthier in many ways than we are, who seem to have so much. While we live in a 'me-first' society, they have community and a profound bond of sisterhood. The simplicity of their lives creates a deep well that is easily filled with love and gratitude, instead of the bottomless pit of lack and comparison I see when visiting people in developed nations.

I left Kenya pondering a deep question: were the women of Korogocho living in captivity and poverty, or were we? Were they like Africa's Big Five roaming the plains of Kenya and we the animals living in zoos in developed cities? Was our life better than theirs, or had we become so accustomed to the flashy glass cages in which we lived that we'd forgotten we were once wild?

A decade later, people would truly come to know what it feels like to live in captivity. Our freedoms were restricted and, in many parts of the world, we were kept within the glass cages of our homes, as the COVID-19 pandemic shook the world and changed our lives forever. People struggled with the challenge of lockdowns and personal restrictions. People lost family members, dear friends, livelihoods and, in many cases, their purpose. So much has been outside of our control. In a state of emergency, decisions are made to keep people safe, not to help people thrive. This is an unprecedented time in our modern society. As governments and health officials tackle the seemingly insurmountable task of mapping our way toward a post-COVID world, individuals must also chart a new course. We must break free from two sets of cages, those that were holding us back before COVID-19 and those that we have built around ourselves during the pandemic. To do so, we need to examine our current mindsets and challenge those perspectives so that we can open ourselves to the possibility of creating a WILD life.

I left Africa with two profound realisations. First, that there are people in the world who need help (and they are not always who or where you might expect them to be) and, second, that I can provide help. I hope this book will be the catalyst for your own profound realisations. I hope you realise there are people in the world who need your help. They are just waiting for you to discover the capacity you have to provide it.

2
Challenge Your Thinking

In this book we'll look at two different ways of seeing the world. For ease of reference, these are the 'WILD Mindset' and the 'Captivity Mindset'. Living a WILD life requires mental flexibility, an open mind, positivity, and the willingness to take risks, hence the WILD Mindset. By comparison a captivity mindset is a closed way of thinking – inherently negative, pessimistic and with a lack mentality.

The first step to transformation is self-awareness and this chapter is designed to challenge your thinking and to shake up some commonly held perspectives. I have no doubt that you will disagree with some, or all, of what follows. Honestly, that's the point. The more resistant you are to an idea, the more closely you should examine your current point of view. You might discover the reason you're still in captivity.

Wealth

How would your life be different if you were insanely wealthy? If money was no object, what dramatic changes would you make in your life? Give up your job? Free yourself from the mundane tasks of the day? Pursue your passion as a humanitarian/ environmentalist/philanthropist?

What if I told you that you are already wealthy?

Just the fact that you're reading this book shows that you've won the lottery. Based on your location and that you have an income, you are likely in the top 10% of the world's wealthiest people. Do a quick search online with the question, 'How rich am I?', enter your income and where you live into the calculator, and it'll give you an understanding of where you sit in relation to the rest of the world.[2] On a global scale, you're likely in the top 10% for income. An individual living in Australia and receiving Centrelink payments (Australian income support) in 2022 is paid almost $17,000 a year. This places them in the top 18% of the world's wealthiest people. Even in a dissatisfying and poorly paid job, you would likely rank higher.

In a global population of billions of people, the vast majority will never outgrow the social circles or financial standings into which they were born. Your economic environment influences every other area

---

2   'How rich am I?', (Giving What We Can, no date), https://
     howrichami.givingwhatwecan.org/how-rich-am-i, accessed
     4 May 2023

of your life – your access to education, where you go to school, your home life, the quality of work that you're able to get, your ability to travel, your access to partners, friends and social circles and your overall quality of life. There's a vast difference in the standard of living for someone in Switzerland versus Ethiopia.[3] When you consider the economic disparity between these countries, you realise how important being born wealthy is to being successful.

What do I mean by this? The 'ultra-wealthy' of the world are not people who work in the corner office, live in mansions and drive Ferraris. They're people like you and me. If you're reading this book, it means you have the money to purchase it and you are educated enough to read it. You are in a privileged position. You are better off than so many around the world. As such, it is our responsibility to do meaningful work with our lives so that our brothers and sisters living in (financially) poorer parts of the world can live a better life tomorrow than they did today.

If you spend your time chasing the money you think you need to feel as though you've made it, you will never achieve what you're really seeking, which is the purpose and fulfilment that comes from being of service. When you focus on your purpose and your service, you will, ironically, be more likely to find the wealth you are seeking – and that might not be money.

---

3   'Standard of living by country: Quality of life by country 2022', (World Population Review, 2022), https://worldpopulationreview. com, accessed 22 May 2022

Proximity is power

The next perspective challenge to face before entering the wild is that your family and friends are the main reason you're not more successful. It might hurt to hear that these people who you love are a big reason why you're not living a WILD life, but proximity equals power. What does that mean? As an example, research has proven that a person's chance of becoming obese increases by 57% if a close friend is obese, 40% if a sibling is obese, and 37% if a spouse is obese.[4] If you're surrounded by people who are depressed and anxious, there's a good chance that you're also feeling that way or are deeply affected by that. If you're surrounded by those who are broke or struggling financially, there's a good chance that you're living pay cheque to pay cheque. You are constantly scanning your social connections for role models of success and failure. Because many of us are surrounded by role models of failure rather than role models for success, you might accept failure as the norm – which it's not. You can choose to model failure or reject it in favour of growth toward success. We can reject the model and create new paradigms while still loving and supporting those close to us.

Interestingly, people who do have successful families sometimes falter beneath their heavy expectations

---

4   'Friends, family can influence your weight—for good or bad', (Harvard T H Chan School, 2014), www.hsph.harvard.edu/news/ hsph-in-the-news/friends-and-family-can-influence-your-weight, accessed 20 April 2023

and harsh judgements. Some of my clients have joked with me, saying their parents told them they could do anything they wanted in life, so long as they were a lawyer, doctor or engineer. While this might have been said half-humorously, it speaks to parents imposing their model of success onto the lives of their children. In these cases, your family's expectations contribute to you not living your best life because you're living *their* idea of what your best life looks like.

Don't get me wrong, in most cases, families love and support each other. Parents have your best interests in mind, but they only know what they know, and the world we're living in today is a different place than it was twenty, thirty or fifty years ago. The way you view and interact with the world would baffle your grandparents. In fact, I often speak to my grandparents about the differences, and they feel that we're living a better lifestyle today in our twenties than they are as retired multimillionaires in their fifties, sixties and seventies. The world has changed at a rapid pace so, while there is wisdom in the advice of experiences from twenty or thirty years ago, it is naïve to think that analogue advice will apply directly to our increasingly digital world. You must be willing to challenge or reject the judgements and expectations of people who care about you to carve out your own path. There's nothing wrong with wanting to make your family proud, unless doing so prevents you from pursuing your best life.

A conversation I had at an event early in my career has always stuck with me. A young woman named

Kimberley came to the event. During one of the breaks, we had the following exchange:

> 'What have you always wanted to do with
> your life?' I asked.

> 'My whole life, I've only had one thing
> I wanted to do, which was to become a dancer.
> I've always loved dancing,' she replied.

> I had to ask, 'So, what are you doing
> right now?'

> 'I'm a naturopath,' she said, looking away.

> 'Wow, okay. Well that's very different,' I said.
> 'Why are you a naturopath and not a dancer?'

> And she replied, 'My dad told me I'm
> too smart to be a dancer and I should do
> something else.'

Because of her father's well-meaning advice, she decided to quit dance and become a naturopath. I'm sure that she was a great naturopath. She was a talented young woman who had dedicated herself to studying and helping others with their health. But you could also tell she was not fulfilled. Because what she loved to do was dance, not practise naturopathy. There's nothing wrong with being a naturopath but you must *want* to be a naturopath. So many of us are doing the 'right thing' according to somebody else, but that 'right thing' may be holding you back from living life on your terms.

When I was getting started in this business, my family (none of whom had gone to university) didn't understand why I would make the investment to get a degree. They didn't know that I was going to be starting my own business. My family, who all love me, care for me and are enormously proud of me, sat me down to discuss my decision. I remember being told that I should get a technical trade so that I had something to fall back on. I vividly recall sitting at the dinner table explaining to them that there was no need for a Plan B because I didn't need any distraction from Plan A.

The best way to help your family change their perspective is by having an honest conversation. Explain to the people you love that you're going to pursue your best life, that you're probably going to make mistakes, but it's important for you to live on your own terms. You must be willing to lose the good opinions of others to create your best life.

The work–life balance myth

The concept of a work–life balance is one of the greatest myths of the modern era. A quick web search delivers more than 1.86 billion results on this topic. What's mind-blowing is that our notions of work and life – and that elusive 'balance' – were created almost

300 years ago to support the rise of the Industrial Revolution.[5] Back then, the original 'working week' saw men, women and even children work up to sixteen hours a day, six days a week. You would have worked Monday to Saturday in hazardous environments within a textile mill, coal mine or steam engine factory. Australia was one of the first societies to push back against labour abuse. By the middle of the nineteenth century, some parts of the country had won the right to an eight-hour work day, but it would take another hundred years before the forty-hour, five-day work week would be established. We were called a 'Workman's Paradise'. Although it was a win for labourers and the general working conditions in our country, the system was not designed for people who are creative, ambitious or driven. The concept was 8 hours of rest, 8 hours of leisure and 8 hours of labour. Today that system feels staggeringly outdated because people are so digitally connected that in reality they often end up working extra hours outside their formal work hours. You try and tell the average employee of a big, multinational corporation who drives to work, complains about the traffic and the cost of parking, and sits in an air-conditioned office all day that he or she is living in a workman's paradise and you'll get some interesting responses.

In truth I'm not actually against a '40-hour work week', but I am against doing something you don't

---

5   Victoria and Albert Museum, 'Industrialization, labor, and life', (*National Geographic*, no date), www.nationalgeographic.org/article/ industrialization-labor-and-life/7th-grade, accessed 17 May 2022

love in exchange for money and living for the weekend, and then calling it work–life balance. I'm sure you'd agree that if you could make the same money you do now, and do what you love on your own terms in your own time from anywhere in the world, you'd take that over the job you have today. Well you can, you just need the right game plan, which we'll cover later.

In 2015 I went to Bali for my mum's fiftieth birthday. We were staying in a family villa and everyone was enjoying a week of relaxation and pampering. Some family members were reading books, some swimming and some getting massages. I was relaxing on the daybed, listening to a webinar about business growth, disruptive technology and the future of the world. To the family, it looked like I was working. On the final day of the trip, Mum sat me down to have a conversation. She expressed, in strong words, how disappointed she was that I had worked while on holiday. It's difficult to understand, until you live it, that there is no separation in my life between work and play, and nor do I want there to be. It's all the same thing – life is life. No one would have questioned me if I had gone out and shopped up a storm or if I'd spent the day drinking at the pool bar. No one would have questioned that because it's part of the normalised concept of downtime or holidaying. I decided to be on my laptop, doing conference calls, checking in with people, watching webinars or upskilling myself – not things most people do on a holiday. Therefore, to Mum, I wasn't on holiday.

The new perspective I suggest you embrace is that there is no boundary between life and work – it is all the same thing. You shouldn't be trying to balance work and life; you should be trying to optimise your work, to allow you to get the most out of life.

Moderation is settling

Do you want to be filthy, stinking rich? At our live events, I often ask the audience for a show of hands in response to that question. The majority respond in the affirmative but about 10–20% of people say no. That 'no' has nothing to do with money; it's based on a desire simply to be content. Their mindset is, 'I want just enough. Money isn't everything and I'm not greedy.'

Consider the choice between being healthy, having a great body and heaps of energy or being sick, overweight and lethargic. Everyone would choose the former. There is no such thing as 'just enough' of a six-pack – you either have one or you don't. Most people just don't want to deal with the pressure of going to the gym or having to summon the dedication to work out. The reality is, you don't want something in moderation; you want to get what you want without having to pay the cost of getting it. Moderation, then, is not a virtue; moderation is the battle cry of mediocrity.

When you start talking about your goals, dreams and bold moves that you are planning, you will face criticism. Beware, once you start getting noticed for being bold, setting goals and implementing the principles of this book, people who love you will tell you to slow down. 'You're so focused / don't get obsessed / take it easy!' They'll warn you about the dangers of taking action, tell you that you're taking too big risks or that you shouldn't have to make hard choices or bold moves to get what you want. They don't want to observe or respect the healthy boundaries you're setting, whether those be around your lifestyle, spending or relationships. The ultimate calling card of someone living a life of mediocrity is when you hear them say, 'Everything in moderation.'

You need to see beyond those kinds of distracting comments. Perhaps you don't have a big or clear enough vision for your life, or maybe you lack people around you who demonstrate how to achieve such a vision easily and effectively. This causes you to associate accomplishing your goals with a tremendous amount of work. Then, when you weigh up the perceived cost, you wonder if it's worth it and settle into limiting beliefs like 'everything in moderation' and 'don't get obsessed'. But if being obsessed with your vision helps you achieve it, why wouldn't you obsess? If you want excellence, if you want to live life on your terms, you must be willing to act when most people are not. I honestly believe that a life of moderation is not a life worth living. Moderate actions, moderate focus and moderate effort will only ever lead to moderate, mediocre outcomes. Do you want a moderate income? Do you want moderate health? Do you want moderate love, intimacy, sex and passion? Do you only want moderate career fulfilment and moderate life purpose?

You can reject moderation and mediocrity. You can go beyond it and infuse every part of your life with WILD success.

You're brainwashed

If you ask people what they want most in life, the Holy Grail answer is happiness. But happiness isn't really the answer. You are conditioned to believe that you want happiness because, for most of your life, marketers have force-fed you bullshit that makes you believe you're not good enough, not successful enough, not attractive enough or happy enough as you are. But, if you were to buy this shiny new thing, you will achieve the happiness that you are chasing. The reality is that a constant state of happiness is a myth, not a goal. What we actually desire, and what we have come to define as happiness, is the feeling of momentum and the sense that our life is progressively improving over time. Or you might have been equating happiness as pleasure, a very different thing.

Most people live in the if/then trap. *If* this particular thing happens, *then* I'll be happy. 'If I make more money, then I'll feel wealthy.' 'If I have these things, then I will feel fulfilled.' The problem is that happiness is not the outcome of those equations. Happiness is not something that you can attain or even something that you should be aiming for. The true secret of happiness isn't in the accomplishment or obtaining of something; rather, it is a by-product of the feeling of progress, the feeling that your life has meaning and that you're contributing to the lives of those around you. If you're not happy in your life, there's nothing wrong with *you* – there's something wrong with your life.

3
Entering The Wild

This book isn't about me, it's about you. That said, I'd like to give you some insight into why these principles are so close to my heart and how my 'WILD life', a life free from captivity, was created. The truth is that the success I have achieved, the lives I have changed and the impact I have made in the world, has very little to do with my own industry or effort and far more to do with the grace and guidance of a loving family, a free country and the opportunity to pursue my wildest dreams

I am fortunate to have been born into a loving, hardworking and entrepreneurial (although it wasn't sexy at the time) family in the northeast of England. If you have children or grandchildren, you'll know what a profound impact they have on how you think about things like the future, your legacy and purpose.

My family was no different. With the addition of the grandchild (that's me) to our family, my grandparents, Ron and Bernadette, started asking themselves hard questions like, 'What do we want for our family's future?' and 'Is the England we know the best place for our children and grandchildren?' Their answers changed the course of my life.

In 1993, Ron and Bernadette made one of the WILDest decisions you could imagine. They left behind their life in the UK, including a home and a successful business, and moved to Australia with just two suitcases, about $10,000 and their youngest child, my aunty. It was a bold choice; they'd never been to Australia, they didn't have a support system, but they went with faith and courage and trusted they would figure it out as they went.

I often say that 'Leaders anticipate and act' and the decision they made is an apt example of this. Gran and Grandad had looked into the future – our future – and decided that the culture and lifestyle we would be exposed to in the northeast of England wouldn't create the wealth of opportunities that they wanted for their family. So they took complete ownership of their family's future and decided to rebuild their life in Australia. Leaving everything behind was no doubt one of the hardest things they had ever done and came with no guarantee of success; nevertheless, they bet on themselves. They slept on the floor for their first few months in Australia while they struggled to find work and rebuild their life. It would be nearly a year before my mum, dad, sister and I made it to Australia and started our new life Down Under. In the years that followed, I watched my grandparents launch businesses, build wealth and create the lifestyle they had always dreamed of for themselves and our family.

Almost three decades later, Ron and Bernadette are retired multimillionaires. They have three wonderful children, six grandchildren and now their first great-grandchild. All the dreams they had envisioned back in the UK have come true, as a result of a relentless work ethic, tremendous belief and faith in themselves and their family.

I have appreciated the sacrifices they made for me and our family from an early age, yet it wasn't until the birth of my own child, Alila Rae, that I fully understood why they needed to make that bold choice. There would be no WILD Success, no financial freedom, no lives changed if there hadn't first been Ron and Bernadette and the WILD decision they made in 1993.

My grandparents have set the precedent for my understanding of what it means to make hard choices. Theirs is a story shared by millions of immigrants around the world who move to Australia, New Zealand, the UK, the USA and many other countries in search of a better life, greater opportunity and the chance to 'make it'.

Think about who has sacrificed for you. Who has given up familiarity and stability for the pursuit of bigger dreams so that you might have a better chance of pursuing your own? Think about that long enough and you'll understand why I do what I do. What my grandparents have done for me means that I *must* succeed. I must thrive, I must endure and I must do whatever I can to make the world a better place. Anything less would be an insult to those who gave up so much to afford me the sacred opportunity to live a WILD life.

Now I'm a parent and life has come full circle. I realise that the person I've become is a by-product of Ron and Bernadette's decisions; in turn, Alila and her children will grow up to be a by-product of mine. Your children and grandchildren will inhabit a world that is shaped in your image. What world will you create for them?

Packing your bags

Now that you're set up to challenge and adapt your thinking, it's time to pack our bags for the journey into the wild. In the world we inhabit, there are irrefutable natural laws, such as the relationship between the moon and tides and the law of gravity. In the same way, there are laws of the wild to be aware of before you begin your journey. We will explore several of these laws in the next part of the book when we delve into the WILD Method. What I want to do now is plant the seeds for the ideas you are about to explore. These are the key elements and concepts that you should keep in mind as you read this book. They are the guideposts to refer to whenever you find yourself in a place of captivity. By learning these laws and living with the mindset they help create, you can open yourself up for the transformations and retransformations you will undergo as you follow the path to the life of your dreams. The laws are:

- **You are responsible for everything in your life.** *You* are in control. You have the ability to respond to any circumstance that may arise. You can choose to do nothing or you can choose to take responsibility and face challenges in order to grow past them. It is up to you to take extreme ownership of the results in your life; take control and create your future.

- **There's no such thing as 'I don't know'.** Throughout this book I'm going to ask you some big questions. How you answer those questions can be life changing. When we're not sure what we want (eg from our career or our relationships), the automatic answer is often, 'I don't know'. The reason you don't know the answer is likely that you have been too afraid to ask yourself the question. Resist that reply.

- **Whatever you believe is true, is true, so choose wisely.** There are no good beliefs and bad beliefs, or positive and negative beliefs; there are only beliefs that serve you and beliefs that don't. It doesn't matter if what you believe is 'true', if it is grounded in fact, or even if it's real. That's the power of belief. So choose your beliefs wisely.

- **You don't see the world as it is, you see the world as you are.** If you want to make changes in your life, you need to clear your mental browser history. You must take control of what you put in your inner search bar. If you're in a cycle of shame and insecurity and you go searching for confidence, you're more likely to find examples of lack of confidence because that's what your brain is currently programmed to look for. To change the world, change who you are; to change who you are, change what you're looking for.

- **What got you here won't get you there.** If you are looking to welcome big changes into your life, you have to reset the way you think about and approach your day-to-day life. Everything in life is a choice and sometimes we need a crisis (a global pandemic will do it) to thrust into the light all the shadowy corners we hadn't previously investigated. What changes have you experienced in your life as a result of the COVID-19 pandemic that you never imagined happening? This is proof that the unimaginable is possible.

- **Where focus goes, energy flows – and results show.** Whatever you focus on will expand; if you're not careful, it will be all that you see in the world. Become discerning about the ideas you feed with your energy and focus, because misery loves company and joy is infectious. In our events we share the 90/10 rule which states, that life is 90% choice and 10% circumstance. Don't live your life as a victim of circumstance. What happens or has happened to you is not your future; it's your past. Your story is not yet finished. Adopt a growth mindset that asks, 'How do I use this experience instead of letting it use me?'

- **Proximity equals power.** We are tribal creatures. There is a part of the brain that is only concerned with our survival. If you model the behaviours of those around you, you are less likely to stand out and so are more likely to survive. In order for you to thrive, it's important to choose your peer group wisely.

- **Success requires obsession; everything in moderation is the battle cry of mediocrity.** The hallmark of successful people is that once they discover what they love to do, they dedicate their life to it. If you want to achieve more in life, become obsessed with doing what you love and watch your success skyrocket.

- **How you do anything is how you do everything.** Understand that how you show up now sets a precedent for how you will continue to show up in the future. We are creatures of habit and the habits you repeat will soon become your autopilot. From today, if you choose to show up deliberately and set a high standard, that behaviour will become the model for the rest of your life.

- **The universe has plans for us that we know very little about.** I believe that there is a 'guiding hand' that has played a part in getting us to this point. There is a bigger purpose and a reason that you're reading these words. Whatever that purpose may be, I'm honoured to be a part of it and hope that the book will be of service to you. I invite you to let more of that divine energy into your life and see what miracles it will bring you.

The next essential step is to get an understanding of your 'WILD'. WILD stands for Wellness, Income, Love and Lifestyle, and Direction. In the following pages, I'm going to expand on each of these key areas of your life. This will help you understand what a life of captivity looks like, not only in terms of mindset or motivation, but also the raw science, the numbers and the reality of living in everyday captivity. This will also give you a glimpse of the future: if you continue to follow the path that everyone else is on, what will your life look like? Together, we'll examine the glass cage keeping you captive and, ultimately, break through it so you can chart a course towards a WILD life – a life lived on your own terms.

Before we go on, complete your own WILD life assessment. There is a short scorecard you can use at www.wildsuccess.global/book, which will help you develop a deeper understanding of where you currently are and what you need to change to start living a WILD life. As we work through each area, you might find that this is the first time you've ever looked so closely at your life. This is a big first step and you should remember three things. First, small changes, when executed every day, add up to make a big impact. Second, seek progress not perfection. Third, you do not have to make this a solo mission. There is nothing wrong with needing a tour guide or a travel companion. As an old African proverb says, 'If you want to go fast, go alone; if you want to go far, go together.'

Let's begin the journey with a rundown of the assessment scorecard. Within your overall WILD Score, you'll have individual scores for each of the five major areas – wellness, income, love, lifestyle and direction. Get clear on your current score and what it means. Zero represents a life of pure captivity, with no freedom, no passion and no positive results in any area; 100% indicates a WILD life, the life of your dreams. For example, if your wellness score is zero, perhaps that means you're living with chronic disease or that your fitness level is at an all-time low. If you're starting at zero, an increase to 50% is a big win. We are aiming to achieve your dream life and rejecting mediocrity, so don't stop there. For you, reaching 100% will represent living your best life, with the body of your dreams, with health, energy and vitality.

This scorecard is your new best friend. You might disagree with me if you're looking at a low number, but don't let it defeat you. You might be freaking out looking at the pieces of your life and saying, 'I didn't realise things were this bad.' That's okay. What matters is that you took the time to look. Understand that clarity equals power because awareness precedes change. Read that again if you need to. You can't change any area of your life if you don't have an awareness of what's not working. That said, working out your WILD Score, whether it's high or low, represents a shift in consciousness that is required to break free from your current captivity. This scorecard is your benchmark for success. You will be able to look back, six months or a year from now, and see how close you are to a free and fulfilling life. The scorecard tool provides some brief 'next steps' to follow that I will expand on as we delve deeper.

To work toward living a WILD life, you must acknowledge that you are living in captivity: that your health, your income, your relationships, your lifestyle and your sense of purpose and direction are not where you want them to be. Over the coming pages, I will help you identify and address the things that aren't working so you can make meaningful progress.

Wellness

We are living amid a national health crisis. In terms of physical health, we are in a situation in Australia where one in four children are overweight or obese and two in three adults are overweight or obese.[6] One in 138,000 people this year will be diagnosed with

---

6   'Overweight and obesity' (2017-2018 financial year), (Australian Bureau of Statistics, 2018), www.abs.gov.au/statistics/health/health-conditions-and-risks/overweight-and-obesity/2017-18, accessed 17 May 2022

cancer. In respect to mental health, one in five Australians has suffered from some form of mental illness in the last 12 months and 44% of Australians will experience some form of mental disorder in their lifetime.[7] Today alone, 178 Australians will try to take their lives[8] and, sadly, eight will succeed.[9] If you find yourself in a position where you're dealing with any of these things, evidently you're not alone. Many people are not operating at their full potential – emotionally, physically, spiritually or financially. The statistics above paint a bleak picture, but we can change it.

By wanting to change and thinking about how you can do it, you're halfway there. To start making changes that will improve your wellness, you must consider how well your body and mind are functioning in five realms: movement, nutrition, recovery, mindset and emotion. First, consider what your current wellness reality is:

1. Are you prioritising physical activity? This can include playing sports, going to the gym, walking, swimming, yoga or anything you do to purposely move your body.

---

7   'Mental health', (Australian Institute of Health and Welfare, no date), www.aihw.gov.au/mental-health/overview/mental-illness, accessed 20 April 2023

8   'Fact sheets', (Suicide Prevention Australia, no date), www.suicidepreventionaust.org/news/statsandfacts, accessed 20 April 2023

9   'Causes of death, Australia', (Australian Bureau of Statistics, 2022), www.abs.gov.au/statistics/health/causes-death/causes-death-australia/latest-release#intentional-self-harm-deaths-suicide-in-australia, accessed 20 April 2022

2. Consider the quality and quantity of food you're putting in your body. Do your eating habits align with your activity levels?

3. Do you take time to rest and recover? Are you prioritising taking care of yourself by monitoring your sleep, mental clarity and energy levels?

4. Do you have a positive outlook on life? How you view the world and the mental self-talk you employ determines your mental health, resilience and overall attitude.

5. Do you process your emotions or do you self-sabotage with, for example, emotional eating or endless social media scrolling?

Many people do not prioritise their health. For example, only 8% of people in Australia reach their daily vegetable intake needs.[10] More concerning, 35% of adults get their daily calories from junk food or highly processed foods and, even worse, this statistic is 41% for children.[11] Remember that our bodies are a snapshot of what we've done in the last three to six months, in terms of eating, moving and thinking. For a child (where six months could be as much as one-eighth of their lives), how can a foundation void of nutrition be expected to result in habits that support a continuing

---

10 'Vegetable consumption', (National Cancer Control Indicators, 2022), https://ncci.canceraustralia.gov.au/prevention/diet/vegetable-consumption, accessed 20 April 2023

11 'Junk food', (Department of Health, Government of West Australia, no date), www.healthywa.wa.gov.au/Articles/J_M/Junk-food, accessed 20 April 2023

healthy lifestyle? These damning statistics only consider the food we ingest. I'm not even touching on the impact of sugar, alcohol or stimulants, all of which are ravaging segments of the population.

Put simply, without good health, you are resigned to sitting on the sidelines of life, paralysed and unable to live up to your full potential.

WILD EXERCISE: Wellness

Based on your scorecard results, write down the changes you need to make immediately regarding your wellness. Frame the questions below within this big-picture question: where will you be one year, three years and ten years from now, if you do not act on these changes?

What changes do you want to make and why? Consider these questions:

- What is your Wellness score (out of 100) and what would you like it to be?
- What does your ideal body look like?
- How far do you like to walk every day?
- What are your biggest wellness challenges (stimulants, alcohol, sugars, other addictions, stress or injury) and do you have a plan for management and recovery?
- What are the positive and negative habits that are responsible for your current wellness snapshot?
- If your body is a reflection of your self-worth and self-esteem, then what does that say about your mindset?
- Has health and fitness been a priority for you and, if not, what's been more important?

Income

The average Australian in 2021 made $1,737.10 a week before tax. The top 1% make more than $237,000 a year. We are all aware of the wealth inequality around the world. In Australia, that inequality sees the wealthiest 20% holding 63% of the country's wealth and the poorest holding less than 1% of the total household wealth.[12]

Looking at the statistics, it's natural to want to criticise the top 1% of earners and those wealthy households but try to refrain from doing so. Most of us have the capacity to increase our income and develop our skills, tools and talents in such a way that we can make $400,000, $600,000 or $1.3 million in a single year. Who wouldn't want to be able to earn that kind of money? Even if you don't need that much to fund your ideal lifestyle, wouldn't it be wonderful to donate to charity or contribute to causes you love and care about? I believe we need to change our relationship with money and our attitude toward wealthy people; we need to move from being critical to being curious.

Consider this: 56% of Australians who are currently part of the workforce do not think they will be able to retire as comfortably as they'd like.[13]

12 'Household income and wealth, Australia (2019–2020 financial year)', (Australian Bureau of Statistics, 2022), www.abs.gov.au/statistics/ economy/finance/household-income-and-wealth-australia/latest-release, accessed 17 May 2022

13 Australian National University Staff, 'Most Aussies say things look dire for when they retire', (ANU, 2021), www.anu.edu.au/news/ all-news/most-aussies-say-things-look-dire-for-when-they-retire, accessed 17 May 2022

They believe they're going to reach retirement age and won't have the ability to self-fund their retirement through superannuation or personal assets. What this means is there's a chance that you will be among the half of Australians who might have to keep working beyond retirement age to pay the bills.

A lot of people delay pursuing their passion in the hope that, when they retire, they will do what they love in their free time. In reality, we know most of us aren't going to get there – we're either going to keep working or rely on a government-funded pension (as I write this book, the current pension model is under strain and could change). If the government reduces or eliminates pensions, you will have to work until you die – unless you have a safety net. Some people will be fortunate enough to live off their principal place of residence. In simple terms, their wealth strategy is to sell the home in which they nurtured their family, downsize and then live off the difference. If you're in that position, I hope you have a big house because downsizing might not provide you with enough cash to fund your retirement.

Imagine for now that you're never going to stop working. You're never going to stop doing what you're doing right now. Does that thought make you want to do something different? Does it motivate you to consider a career change? Would you finally make your passions a priority, if the alternative was doing unsatisfactory work just to earn a pay cheque, indefinitely? You might as well pursue that passion now to avoid that alternative depressing economic reality.

I believe that financial abundance is available to anyone who identifies their passions, cultivates skill and dedicates their life to sharing it with others. You can set your sights above the middle class, but that requires proactive moves on your part. If you don't surround yourself with wealthy people, you'll never be wealthy yourself. If you spend more than you earn, you'll always be broke and in debt. If you spend more time watching TV than you do learning and investing in yourself, neither you nor your income will grow.

No matter how motivated, driven or confident you are in your own abilities, if you're part of that median-earner statistic, you have to do something completely different to become financially free. That will involve completely rejecting the system that is keeping you in captivity. Instead, you need to set the game up for you to win. Jim Rohn, the American entrepreneur, author and motivational speaker, once said that you get paid based on the value you bring to the marketplace.[14] How can you bring more value to your marketplace?

WILD EXERCISE: Income

Do you have a negative relationship with money? Are you always feeling badly about how much money you have and that there's not enough? Are you in a position where your beliefs about money are holding you back?

---

14 'Jim Rohn: Increasing Your your value to the marketplace' (YouTube, no date), www.youtube.com/watch?v=04_8eqr86LU, accessed 20 April 2023

Again, frame the questions below within this big-picture question from the perspective of income: where will you be one year, three years and ten years from now if you do not act?

- What is your Income score (out of 100) and where do you want it to be?
- How much money are you making right now?
- What are you doing for work?
- What would your dream life require you to earn in relation to your current income?
- Could you increase your income by changing jobs or moving into a different industry?
- Do you have the skills, tools and talents that are required for success in today's employment market?
- Are you upskilling and leveraging to make yourself more valuable?
- Do you seek out networking opportunities with peers who are successful in your dream job?

Love

How many people do you know who are living a passionate, loving and fulfilling life with their significant other and have remained committed to that relationship long term? It's what we all want, yet it's hard to find and even harder to keep. Why?

The world we live in today is incredibly complex. From a single person's perspective, we have access to more than half of the world's population via social media,[15] so the dating pool has never been wider, but that also means the temptation has never been greater. For couples in a relationship, less and less time is being spent together while we climb the corporate ladder, so our free time is dwindling. Add the financial pressure that is crippling many people and it is understandable that new relationships are harder to forge. With these same indicators in mind, it's no surprise that more than 43% of marriages in Australia fail.[16]

Given these statistics, the motivations for marriage are interesting. You would never go to Apple or Samsung to buy a mobile phone if it broke 50% of the time. Who in their right mind would sign a contract knowing that, if the product broke, it would cost you tens of thousands of dollars and, in many cases, half of your assets? You would never consider an upgrade if the second phone came with a 65% chance of failure. Sadly, the chances of finding a marriage that works don't improve the more times you try. For so many couples, they see the only solution as divorce. According to *Money* magazine, the average divorce can take three years and cost each party $50,000–$100,000, and that's just in legal fees.[17] Imagine instead investing three

15 Chaffey, D, 'Global social media statistics research summary 2022', (Smart Insights, 2022), www.smartinsights.com/social-media-marketing/social-media-strategy/new-global-social-media-research, accessed 22 May 2023

16 Bechara, S, 'Marriage and divorce rates and statistics in Australia 2022', (Unified Lawyers, updated 4 February 2022), www.unifiedlawyers.com.au/blog/marriage-divorce-rates-statistics/ accessed 22 May 2022

17 Trainor, T, 'How to save tens of thousands on the cost of your divorce', (*Money*, 2017), www.moneymag.com.au/save-thousands-divorce, accessed 26 April 2023

years into improving yourself and your marriage, and spending half that money on personal growth. Your relationship would be unrecognisable! I believe we need to find a new way of approaching love, intimacy and connection.

A lot of people I speak with tell me they are only staying in their relationship until the kids graduate from school, until things settle down or until that 'someday' when it gets better. But what if 'someday' never comes? There's a good chance your relationship is going to stay the same or get worse because, after the age of thirty, 95% of our neurological pathways are pre-set.[18] This means that romantic partners who haven't yet struck the right balance aren't going to, unless they're prepared to habitually work on themselves and the relationship.

If you're in a struggling relationship, ask yourself: are you *both* prepared to work on it? If you're single, consider: are you hiding behind your 'single and happy' status because you're avoiding another failed relationship? You may indeed be happy single, but many use that as a justification for not putting themselves out there, when in truth they're just scared of being hurt again.

If you're not clearing past baggage, you're going to keep attracting the same people. In this area of your life, change cannot happen until you've learned the lessons from your experiences and put effort into

---

18   Giang, V, 'What it takes to change your brain's patterns after age 25', (Fast Company, 2015), www.fastcompany.com/3045424/ what-it-takes-to-change-your-brains-patterns-after-age-25, accessed 20 June 2021

improving your relationship with yourself. If you're single, you can take this as the sign you've been waiting for – now is the time to invest in yourself. Being the best version of yourself is the way to find the best partner for the long term. If you're married, also take this as the sign you've been waiting for – now is the time to invest in your marriage. Individuals who work on themselves and bring authentic, intentional communication to their relationship have the tools to overcome the challenges that all relationships face.

WILD EXERCISE: Love

You need to create powerful habits and rituals to make sure you are always aiming to be the best version of yourself every day, for yourself and for your partner. Again, frame the questions below from the perspective of love: where will you be one year, three years and ten years from now if you do not act?

- What is your Love score (out of 100) and where do you want it to be?
- Are you in a passionate, loving and committed relationship?
- Do you have role models of successful relationships in your life?
- Do both parties support each other's highest and truest values?
- Do you know what your highest and truest values are?
- Are you in a relationship of circumstance and convenience, or of purpose and passion?

- Do you make time in your day or week to discuss your relationship with your partner?
- Do you actively find ways to grow and nurture your relationship?

Lifestyle

According to Qualtrics (an American experience management company), an astonishing 69% of Western employees report being disengaged at work. Many Australians are working for a pay cheque, not for passion.[19] Think about how many people preach work–life balance yet are working forty- or fifty-hour work weeks. When you factor in the commute, most of these people are spending sixty to seventy hours of their week doing something they don't love. No wonder so many people feel like they are living a less than satisfactory lifestyle.

Let's say you get four weeks of holiday a year. You spend those weeks trying to cram in all the activities you love to do with all the people you love to do them with, only to return to work exhausted and you repeat the cycle the next time 'holidays' roll around. Clearly, this definition of work–life balance was designed by employers focused on their bottom line, not by

---

19 Hilton, J, 'How engaged are your employees?', (Human Resources Director, 2020), www.hcamag.com/au/specialisation/industrial-relations/how-engaged-are-your-employees/212335, accessed 21 June 2021

human beings focused on filling their days with love and purpose.

Operating under this ruse of work–life balance, you're constantly living life on somebody else's terms. It's often said that if you don't put your priorities in your schedule, somebody else will schedule in theirs. When your schedule is filled with tasks that don't align with your higher purpose, you will find yourself moving further away from your ideal lifestyle. If you're not actively constructing the lifestyle of your dreams, you're never going to have it. You must intentionally design your life around your goals, not try to fit your goals around your life.

WILD EXERCISE: Lifestyle

Most people live each day fuelled by caffeine, nicotine and food, not by their passion. If you don't make a bold change right now, what does your lifestyle look like one year, three years and ten years from now?

- What is your Lifestyle score (out of 100) and what do you want it to be?
- Are you doing work you love to do?
- Is your work just convenient, or is it deliberate and intentional?
- Are you living in an environment you find beautiful and inspiring?
- Are you surrounded by people who love their work?
- Do you make time to do the things you really want to do?

- How do you prioritise your passions with what you do for a living?
- Would it be easy for you to move to another country and generate income?

Direction

Finally, let's talk about direction and purpose. Many people who come to me for support and guidance are looking to find their purpose and gain a sense of direction. In today's world of distractions, people are feeling overwhelmed and lost. With a laundry list of vices and distractions such as alcohol, gambling, porn, self-harm, food, violence, drugs and over-work, who can focus on their truest and highest calling? People are distracted because they have not yet learned how to push aside the clutter and focus on their life's meaning and purpose. Their days are wasted on empty pursuits instead of being filled with activities that bring joy to their lives. Most people have no idea where they're going in life because they've never stopped to ask themselves where they want to be. In our programmes, we spend three to five hours getting clear on where you want to go with the rest of your life. We don't try to find that within your current reality; rather, we design it by determining your dream life and then reverse-engineering from there.

Many people are lost and searching for more, but they feel debilitated, inadequate and stuck because they lack a deep, meaningful purpose. There has been a gradual but significant disconnection from religion in recent years. Once, people found purpose and meaning in their faith and their way of life was largely dictated by the religion they followed. Today, we are more likely to find purpose in our work than in a higher power.

While religious affiliation has been on the decline, there has been a sharp rise in consumerism. In order to fill the void, people are buying flashy cars, watches, jewellery, designer clothes, luxury holidays, nice houses and shiny objects. Increasingly, it seems we're living in a world that is focused more on vanity than substance and clarity. If you can see that you're filling your life with distractions, now is the time to bring more focus and direction to your life.

WILD EXERCISE: Direction

It is a simple truth that if you believe your life has purpose and meaning, it does. But if you feel your life is meaningless, that might be one of the reasons you lack direction. If nothing changes in regard to your direction, where will your life be one, three and ten years from now? 'I don't know' is probably going to be your answer.

- What is your Direction score (out of 100) and what do you want it to be?
- What distractions are holding you back?
- Do you prioritise the things in your life that you want to do and say no to the rest?
- Do you have people around you who are big thinkers and encourage you to consider great ideas?

- Is your career a reflection of what you believe you're put on the planet to do?
- Do you have a clear plan that will take you from where you are now to where you want to go?
- Do you measure and track the progress you're making every single day?
- Do you feel as though you are being guided through the world you live in and that you are here with a higher purpose and a higher calling?

PART TWO
BREAKING FREE

4

The WILD Method

Completing your WILD Scorecard shines a spotlight on your opportunity areas. Bringing focus to these areas allows you to identify your current barriers and the work you need to do in order to live your WILD life. If we were to compare where we are on this journey to climbing Mount Everest, we'd be at base camp. The real work and the real reward come from following the WILD Method. This is the signature process that I've developed over the past decade of working with hundreds of thousands of people like you. Following this method will bring understanding to the challenges and barriers you face and instigate action toward achieving your goals and aspirations. The WILD Method reliably helps you to create the game plan that will bridge the gap between the life you are living today and the life of your dreams. A phenomenal future lies ahead. When you reach the summit of your mountain and the light touches the huge landscape stretching out in front of you, you will feel the enormity of the rewards for the effort you are about to undertake.

Let's dive in. To master any area of your life, you need three things: to have a compelling vision, to create internal alignment and to develop a proven strategy. Think of the WILD Method as a formula for success. It looks like this:

Compelling Vision + Internal Alignment
+ Proven Strategy = WILD Success

Like any equation, finding the unknown quantity, whatever that element is for you, is the challenge but, once you fill in the blanks, WILD Success is the answer.

Compelling vision

The first step of the WILD Method is to create a compelling vision. I often say that if you don't know where you're going, chances are you're going to get lost. Certainly, many people feel like they are going around in circles – perhaps because they are.

There have been studies on how people navigate through dense rainforests or expansive deserts when walking on foot and without a map. During the day, they can easily navigate the world around them because they have clarity of vision. When they can see where they are and where they want to go, they walk in a straight line. However, when the sun sets and it grows dark, they lose their bearings and walk in circles until the sun rises and they regain their vision.[20]

If you feel as though you have been walking in circles and are frustrated with your lack of progress, know that most people would keep walking around in circles. The distinction between you and them is that you looked up, saw the pattern and realised the need to change.

To get back on track, you need clarity about what you want from your life. This is not what you *think* you can achieve; it is what you *truly* desire. When creating a compelling vision for your future, it needs to be based upon desire and possibility, not reality. Whether you think you can achieve it or not, design a game plan around what you really want. Don't waste your time trying to perfect smaller things when you could be focusing on the big picture.

Les Brown, one of the most well-known motivational speakers in the world, said, 'The reason why most people fail in life is not that they aim too high and they miss, but because they aim too low and they hit.'[21] This is the result of underestimating yourself. When you set out with no destination in mind, no matter where you end up, it feels like you failed. Let's say

---

20 Cox, L, 'People do walk in circles when they're lost', (abc News, 2009), https://abcnews.go.com/Health/MindMoodNews/study-shows-people-walk-circles-woods/story?id=8368583, accessed 20 April 2023

21 'Les Brown: Why people fail', (YouTube, no date), www.youtube.com/watch?v=uekdv8SiTec, accessed 20 April 2023

you really wanted to be a marine biologist as a kid. Instead of staying focused on that vision, you prioritised playing video games and now you work at a pet store, cleaning goldfish tanks. You think back to your marine biologist dream and wonder where you went wrong. You have a laundry list of excuses: that you're tired, you're bored, you're stuck, you're uninspired, uncommitted and, many people might say (or you might have said to yourself in your darker moments) that you're lacking the clarity of purpose you need to find the right direction.

In one of my favourite movie scenes, from *Alice in Wonderland*, Alice is walking through a maze and finds herself lost in the middle of a forest. There are so many different paths to take that she hesitates and asks the Cheshire Cat where she should go. The cat asks her where she wants to be – Alice says that it doesn't matter, so the cat replies that in that case it doesn't matter which way she goes.

Many people hesitate at the crossroads of their life because they don't want to make the wrong decision. They don't realise how dangerous that indecision is. Commit this to memory: *indecision will cost you more than the wrong decision*. A wrong decision can provide a valuable lesson; when you don't decide, when you hesitate, you miss out on the value of experience and wisdom, which only leads to more hesitation. So let's get clear on where you want to go. One way to achieve clarity of vision is to complete the below exercise.

WILD EXERCISE: Perfect day

Visualise yourself, ten years from now, living your perfect day. You wake up and you're ready to do amazing things with your life. You're surrounded by like-minded, inspirational people who have beautiful hearts and souls. You're contributing and serving those in your circle, your community and beyond. Take some time now to centre yourself and get clear on what you really want from your life.

To help sharpen this vision, ask yourself these questions:

- Who is with you? Who are the people in your circle of family, friends and relationships?
- What is most important to you when you consider your perfect day?
- What are you doing with your day? Where are you working? How are you spending your time?
- How are you learning and experiencing the world? Are you reading, attending workshops, travelling?
- How are you serving and giving back? Are you involved with a charity, or do you volunteer your time to a community organisation?
- How are you ensuring you are living your dream life? Do you start this day with goal-setting, journaling or speaking to a coach or mentor?

Designing your perfect day this way is important because it allows you to reverse-engineer the process of getting there. For a free guided meditation audio that can help you with this activity, visit our website at www.wildsuccess.global/book. The meditation will

> help you identify the area of your life where you most require clarity and help develop the compelling vision that you want to create.

A word of warning: before you begin using the WILD Method, a paradigm shift is required. Remember, the reason most people never achieve their goals is because they set them based on their current reality, based on what they think is achievable, not on what they desire. I've come to realise that the hallmark of successful people is that they find a way to raise their reality to the level of their dreams, whereas unsuccessful people lower their dreams to match their reality.

Your dream life

On 20 February 2018, as the sun set on one of the most magical evenings in the Maldives, I asked my best friend and soulmate, Ash, to marry me. With some convincing, coaching and neuro-linguistic programming (NLP) – I will elaborate on this later in the book – she said yes. After the excitement of calling and telling our families the big news, we began the journey of planning our wedding. Sitting in the Maldives, soaking up this incredible moment in our lives while admiring the beautiful, crystal clear water in front of us, I thought about our upcoming wedding day, where it would take place and how we wanted to celebrate. As we shared our thoughts with each other, we realised that we didn't just want to get married, we wanted to create an experience that our friends and family would never forget. As we sat dreaming and discussing, I had a crazy idea. What if we got married here, in the Maldives? 'Impossible,' was my first thought. The Maldives is expensive, with accommodation costing at least US$1,000 a night plus transfers to the island of US$500 a person. Not to mention we had just paid US$18 for an espresso. Needless to say, a wedding here would be way beyond our budget. We didn't want to elope, though. We wanted to create something magical both for us and for those we loved most.

We decided to pose a hypothetical question: what if we could get all our friends and family to the Maldives for the same price that we'd pay for a wedding in Australia? What if it *was* possible? In that circumstance, of course we'd get married in the Maldives, but did that possibility exist? We had no idea, but I was committed to exploring the options. Surely there was a location somewhere in the Maldives that could offer what we wanted within our budget. Certainly, it would be worthwhile to ask. The worst that could happen was that we'd realise it wasn't possible so, upon our return, I began working on our dream. Within a matter of weeks, we were able to identify an island that could accommodate what we were looking for. For roughly the cost of a big Australian wedding, we were able to host more than thirty of our friends and family in the Maldives, at an all-inclusive resort, to celebrate our special day. We were so excited that we put down a deposit and got our family together to share the big news. I've known for a long time that the only way to make things happen is to leverage yourself and force yourself to expand, so that's what we did. Even though I'd placed only a small deposit, I told all our family that we had already paid for the entire wedding and that they were all staying, at our expense, in the Maldives for five nights to celebrate our wedding day. If they covered their flights, we'd cover the rest. Our families were ecstatic (aside from the 'you should be saving for a family' conversations) and I had all the leverage I needed to get to work. We immediately set up a payment plan with the hotel and started arranging everything we needed to make the day just as special as we had dreamed.

With the wedding planned for February the following year, Ash suggested that we visit the island while returning from a work trip to Europe. We could meet the staff and see the island where we'd say 'I do'. In September 2018, four and a half months before our big day, we landed in the Maldives for what should have been a lovely tour of the island.

Have you ever stayed somewhere that looked amazing online but, in real life, was awful? Well, then you know how we felt when we rocked up to our dream wedding destination, turned spring-break backpackers' hostel, in the Maldives. The photos and reviews online were great but the reality was terrible. Ash sat on the beach after the tour and cried. We'd already paid tens of thousands of dollars, our families had booked flights and now our dream wedding was hanging by a thread with only a few months to go.

We decided to use the time we had left in the Maldives to see as many islands as possible, hoping we'd find one that was in our budget (after losing all the money we'd already paid) and matched the vision we had for our special day. In theory, this sounds simple enough but, practically and logistically, it was a nightmare. The Maldives is a collection of about 1,200 tiny islands scattered over a vast distance. Most are accessible only by seaplane and to travel between them you have to return to the capital Malé and wait for that specific island's private charter. The process is as time-consuming as it is expensive, with each trip costing more than US$500 a person – money that we didn't have.

We managed to visit seven islands over three days, some for only fifteen minutes. On the last island, Adaaran Select Hudhuranfushi, we found what we were looking for. After some back and forth, we managed to arrange an incredible five nights of luxury for our families and friends in over-water villas. Now, we just had to pay for it all.

Once we'd cancelled the previous resort, we lost our deposit and had to start from scratch with a new island and new plan. The weeks that followed took everything we had. I still remember Ash breaking down in tears one morning. 'What if we can't pull it off?' she said. 'What if we can't pay for the wedding? Should we just cancel and do something low-key here in Perth?' I've always believed that doubt kills more dreams than failure ever could and, while we were a long way from victory, we hadn't failed yet.

We decided that we would do everything in our power between that moment and the minute we left for the airport to make our dream wedding happen. If the taxi pulled up and we hadn't paid for the wedding, we'd call the family, tell them we'd failed and that we'd be getting married in our backyard. Until that final moment, though, we'd give it our all. Our taxi was booked for Saturday 16 February and on Monday 11 February, we still needed to scrape together more than $35,000.

On Wednesday 13 February, less than a week to our wedding day, I got a call from a client who said he'd wired me the $5,000 deposit for a coaching programme. This was the final piece of the puzzle. It meant we'd hit our target and secured the money we needed to do what had seemed impossible. We were going to the Maldives and we were going to get married.

Looking back on that time now, I can barely remember the stress, pressure and sleepless nights. What I'll always remember, though, is the look on our loved ones' faces when they drove up the jetty to the cluster of over-water villas we'd booked for them. They say money can't buy happiness, but this came close. The thing is, it wasn't only money that bought this experience. It all started with a bold goal, a compelling vision and the courage to risk failure in search of the magnificent. There were many times where we could, and probably should, have called off this crazy plan. But we persisted. We never let doubt hold us back from our dreams. This is the same attitude you must take in the pursuit of your vision in life. When I look back, I realise that experience wasn't made magnificent by the Maldives or the villas, but in its representation of what's possible; of what can happen when you go after what you want in life.

Most people don't give themselves the opportunity to fail. They give up on their dreams, without even trying, because they don't believe they can achieve them. Don't settle for aiming for only slightly more than you already have. When in doubt, be bold.

Now let's look at your dream life, the life you're going to create for yourself and those you love.

WILD EXERCISE: Dream life

The best way to predict the future is to create it. Think about where you want to get to over the next ten years. Write down some of your goals or intentions in the following three areas:

Dream Life	Ten Years
GROWTH	
(How do you want to grow?)	
CONTRIBUTION	
(How do you want to contribute?)	
EXPERIENCES	
(What major life experiences do you want to have?)	

When you're imagining yourself living the life of your dreams ten years from now, consider how you want to have grown, both personally and professionally. How do you see yourself contributing at work, at home and within your community? List your big-ticket items. Do you want to experience being of service, travelling, learning a new skill, starting a new relationship or changing careers?

Now that you have clarity about creating your compelling vision, we can move on to find the elements that will bring you internal alignment. Together, we can figure out how your beliefs and emotions, supported by your habits and focus, can create the alignment required to transform your dreams into reality.

Interview: Hanalei Swan

Devastatingly impacted by the 2008 global financial crisis, Hanalei's parents refused to accept defeat. Rather, they looked at the pieces of their broken life as an opportunity to build the life of their dreams. This decision carved a unique path for their infant daughter. In her early formative years, Hanalei was shaped by the experience of global travel and the influence of entrepreneurs. The result is a young woman who has not waited to 'grow up' to start living life on her own terms. With the help of her parents and a well-met mentor, Hanalei is, at age fourteen, an artist, fashion designer, international speaker and author.

With what she has been able to accomplish at such a young age, Hanalei personifies the benefits of being born into a WILD life. Her play-time artistic endeavours grew into fashion designs. Her experiences of being and speaking on stage in a room full of interesting people prepared her to become an international speaker. Her parents' encouragement toward, and inclusion in, the world of business has seen her diversify her skills and talents to include the title of author among her many accomplishments.

I spoke with Hanalei to better understand how the lifestyle her parents chose shaped her and how she was able to identify and harness the compelling vision that she was born with.

Calvin: What does 'living a WILD life' mean to you?

Hanalei: I've grown up differently than most kids but, for me, this has always been normal. A lot of people ask me, 'How does it feel travelling so much? And why have you done this?' Or 'What's that feeling you get?' And the questions almost come from a place of it being unnatural. To me, travelling and stepping outside the box is normal. I'm constantly exposed to change and new opportunities and I've had to learn how to adapt to that. It can be an odd concept for other people because they didn't grow up with it. But I've been exposed to it from a really young age. I've made my own decisions and learned to be independent. I've grown up living this wild lifestyle, so I understand that the environment that surrounds you is what builds you. It builds the foundation and lays the first stepping stones for who you are as a person.

Calvin: How did you first identify your passions and talents to create a compelling vision for your life?

Hanalei: I remember this one crucial moment so well. Me and my mum were walking on the beach one day and she asked me, 'What do you want to be now?' instead of, 'What do you want to be when you grow up?' That was a big turning point for me because, even as a seven-year-old, even as someone super-young, it sparked ideas in my head. Being asked what I wanted to be *now* was a huge moment for me. I remember thinking, 'Wow, I can actually do something now – I don't have to wait.'

I feel finding my passion was easier because my parents always exposed me to new things. They supported and guided me by saying, 'Sure, if you want to try this, do it.' My family always had this open mindset about learning. If you are excited and if you think it's interesting, go learn about it. So when I was asked what I want to be now, I realised, 'Wow, I can do so many things.' I started listing things like, 'I want to be a photographer and take photos just like some of my favourite people do.' And then I thought, 'Oh, I want to be an artist,' and 'I want to be a fashion designer.' And the fashion designer idea actually stuck. My mum had filmed this conversation at the time and I remember re-watching the video a few years later and seeing how far I'd come. Remembering speaking those words out loud was almost a form of affirmation, of saying, 'This is who I am. This is what I am,' instead of, 'One day I'm going to do this.'

Calvin: How did you get from the idea of, 'This is what I think I was put on the planet to do,' to 'This is what I do'? And what is your recommendation for someone who is trying to make that big shift?

Hanalei: The first thing is, don't compare yourself or your journey to anyone else's because their journey is different to yours. We all have grown and we all have had similar struggles in different stories. Now, based on who you are, separate from anyone else's experience or expectation, you can make a change at any time. You just need to find that change. If you really want to go for something, you really want to act on something, you can. It's about how you weave it into your life by trying something new or learning something new. No matter what age you are, what type of person you are or how your life has gone, you can make that change if you commit to it. A lot of times people say, 'I don't have enough money' or 'I can't do this because of my family' or 'I can't do this because blah, blah, blah.' Those perspectives of negativity prevent you from finding a solution because you're just stating a problem. Instead of, 'I don't have enough money,' try, 'I need to figure out a new way to make money if I really want to do this.' If you want to accomplish something, you'll find ways to weave around your obstacles and instead grow toward what drives you. When you find yourself saying, 'I can do this if I want,' then you've found your passion, you will find a way to strive and find that drive to learn something. You'll find a way to make that happen.

The second thing is to have a conversation with yourself about what will make you happy. Ask yourself, 'What do you want to be now?' Are you happy with where you're at in life? Is this the person that you want to be? Are you content with who you are? Are you content with what you're doing?' And if you're not, then identify what could change that. What are the things that you need to change to find that happiness?

5
Internal Alignment

Have you ever felt like you're taking one step forward only to end up taking two steps back? Then you know how it feels to experience self-sabotage.

Now that you have a compelling vision, the next step is to understand and develop your internal alignment. Over the past five years of holding events, working with clients and listening to their stories, I've come across a long list of challenges that hold people back from achieving their goals. Generally, these can be categorised into four broad areas:

1. Lack of belief

2. Negative emotions

3. Sabotaging behaviours

4. Obscured focus

It's likely that you can relate to one (or four) of these areas. We all have beliefs, we all experience emotions, we all have effective or ineffective habits and, in the world of social media, we all sometimes struggle to maintain focus. I am going to help you understand why these four challenges block progress and teach you the skills you'll need to install unshakeable self-belief, emotional mastery, powerful behaviours and an obsessive focus.

The explanations and exercises provided will help you complete an internal audit. I will repeat this more than once in the pages ahead because it is a useful mantra: awareness precedes change. Bringing awareness to your challenges is the most direct way to change whatever is preventing you from achieving your life goals. The self-awareness you will cultivate by working on your internal alignment is crucial for following through on your goals. Whether you have a wellness goal of going to the gym and eating healthier foods, a financial goal of saving money, a lifestyle goal of getting up early, a relationship goal of putting yourself out there or you are simply searching for more direction in your life, those goals will never become your reality if you lack internal alignment. You will find yourself blocked by negative emotions such as fear and doubt, or you will allow yourself to engage in limiting behaviours when you know there is a better option.

Let's get started on creating internal alignment by looking at the first element, which is creating unshakeable self-belief.

Unshakeable self-belief

Do you believe in yourself – like, really believe in yourself? As actor Will Smith once said, 'The first step before anyone else in the world believes it, is that you have to believe it.'[22]

I've seen first-hand that most people have a massive belief deficiency. Your self-belief determines the actions that you take in every area of your life. No one knows what's possible in their lives or the extent of their emotional, physical or financial limits, so you need to choose your beliefs wisely. As pioneering car manufacturer Henry Ford is reported to have said, 'Whether you think you can or you can't, you're usually right.'

When I was fifteen I had a moment of awareness where I realised that everyone around me fell into two categories: those who *believed* they were capable of much less than they really were or those who *believed* they were capable of much more. And perhaps even more importantly, either way, they were all probably wrong. I understood then that true capability wasn't what mattered, what was important was what people believed to be true. I made a decision in that moment to believe I was capable of more than I really was and, as a result, I know my life has been completely different to what it would have been if I'd decided the other way.

---

22 'Will Smith: Mindset wisdom', (YouTube, no date), www.youtube. com/watch?v=XkziAM_ZyDM, accessed 20 April 2023

Core beliefs are formed during the initial years of our life and begin to cement into our subconscious mind from 7 years old.[23] The beliefs introduced to us during this time are modelled on our parents, loved ones and social environments. In the years leading up to adulthood, these beliefs are either challenged and broken or they're reinforced. If, for example, you are born into a religious family that attends church and engages in a religious practice, in the subsequent years spent at high school and university, learning about the world outside the family home, that religious foundation may be challenged. At this intersection, you either find yourself gradually deconstructing your religious beliefs or they become reinforced. If beliefs are unquestioned, they will become unconscious and ultimately, your truth. You start to identify things in the world as not just a belief but as a universal truth.

How beliefs are formed

Consider the fact that the earth is round. The idea was first proposed and became accepted over time but most of us have never physically seen the full curvature of the earth. Very few people have had the opportunity to see our planet from space and visually validate that fact. Explorers and scientists have confirmed it as scientific fact, so we embrace the idea as truth. This is not a limiting belief.

---

23 Wilson Jr, RE, 'Are negative core beliefs wrecking your life?', (*Psychology Today*, 2021), www.psychologytoday.com/us/blog/the-main-ingredient/202109/are-negative-core-beliefs-wrecking-your-life, accessed 20 April 2023

Another example is the knowledge that water is made up of hydrogen and oxygen. Unless we are scientists, most of us don't have a detailed understanding of what hydrogen and oxygen are or how they combine at a molecular level to make water, we just know that they do. The construct we've created in our minds is accepted as accurate and we don't challenge it. Or consider the concept of time. At some point, there was no construct of a twenty-four-hour day or a seven-day week. We invented those principles and concepts by looking at the world around us and codifying patterns we saw.

These examples illustrate how we unconsciously accept certain ideas about our world as true, meaning they become unquestioned and unconscious beliefs. While in some cases this is fine, when it comes to beliefs about ourselves, this can be limiting. There are beliefs in our lives that we have held for so long, we don't stop to question why we have them or where they came from.

Imagine for a moment that you were born with the belief that you are here to make a difference in the world. Take a moment to think about how different your life would be if you had been born with that fundamental belief in yourself. I was raised, practically from the moment of my conception, to believe that I was put on this earth to make a difference. My gran, Elizabeth Coyles, is a medium. Going back to before I was born, she would travel around the UK to host readings. A reading is an open session where she would channel messages from spirits intended for the people in her audience. In the late 1980s, she began receiving a message that there was a child coming but no one in her audiences seemed to connect to that message. The message kept coming back, incessantly, that there was a child, the child was a boy, and had a purpose; he had a mission to change the world.

Not long after these messages began, both her sons learned that they were expecting their first child. On 17 April, as Gran and Grandad headed to the hospital to welcome me into the world, story has it that a rainbow appeared over Sunderland General Hospital and Elizabeth realised that the messages were about me. Since the moment of my birth, I have lived within that belief that I am here to change the world and to make it a better place. The life decisions I make and have made come from that place, that belief system. Right or wrong, true or false, reality or make-believe, just consider how different your life would be if you were born into that story? Imagine, for example, the anxiety and pressure young people feel today when considering what they want to be when they grow up. Imagine the pressure they feel making big decisions about the rest of their life when they are barely even adults. Now consider that I didn't feel any of that. I'm here to change the world, after all, so careers and pathways and tests don't matter. I'm here for much bigger things. After failures and setbacks, I would just keep moving forward because I believed, and still believe, that I am on this earth for a purpose much greater than any exam or test. These hurdles, which can slowly chip away at a young person's self-belief, were just minor irritations to me. My focus was on a greater mission.

What are the minor things you focus on that drain your energy, distract you from your purpose and erode your self-confidence?

Why your beliefs matter

Let's look at the science around beliefs. Research suggests that the quality of your beliefs can help you live longer. In one study, middle-aged adults who had a positive outlook on their life lived an average of 7.6 years longer than those who had limiting beliefs.[24] In a New Zealand study, researchers found that after adjusting for social class, IQ, depression and body mass index, adolescents with low self-confidence or low self-esteem were at an increased risk of poverty, criminal activity and poor mental and/or physical health by their mid-twenties.[25] Both genders are impacted, with proof found in a study of nine- to eleven-year-old boys in Florida, showing that those with self-esteem issues had a 60% higher rate of drug dependency ten years later,[26] while other studies

---

24 Levy, BR, Slade, MD, Kunkel, SR, and Kasl, SV, 'Longevity increased by positive self-perceptions of aging', *Journal of Personality and Social Psychology*, 83/2 (2002), 261–270, https://pubmed.ncbi.nlm.nih.gov/12150226, accessed 20 April 2023

25 Poulton, R, Caspi A, Milne, BJ, Thomson, WM, Taylor, A, Sears, MR, and Moffitt, T, 'Association between children's experience of socioeconomic disadvantage and adult health: A life-course study', *The Lancet*, 360/9346 (2002), 1640–1645, www.thelancet.com/journals/lancet/article/PIIS0140-6736(02)11602-3/fulltext, accessed 20 April 2023

26 Conrad Stoppler, M, 'Low self-esteem may lead to drug abuse in boys', (Medicine Net, no date), www.medicinenet.com/low_self-esteem_may_lead_to_drug_abuse_in_boys/views.htm, accessed 17 June 2021

found that girls with high self-esteem were less likely to develop bulimia.[27]

People with high self-esteem are happier, more likely to undertake difficult tasks and persist longer in the face of failure. The more they challenge themselves, the quicker they recover from disasters; they might also be quicker to identify hopeless enterprises too. They have a decreased risk of heart disease and a stronger immune system, all based on their self-esteem, self-confidence and ability to believe in themselves.[28]

There is overwhelming evidence that your sense of self-belief is directly linked to your pay cheque. Dr Martin Seligman, known for his theories on positive psychology, found that optimists make more money and are more loyal. In a study of the life insurance industry, Seligman found that optimistic salespeople sold 88% more insurance than their pessimistic colleagues. The study also indicated that agents in the least optimistic quarter of respondents were three times more likely to quit than those in the most optimistic quarter.[29]

27 Fremder, CB, 'Self-esteem and eating disorders as related to gender', (*Scholars' Journal of Undergraduate Research*, McKendree University, Issue 18), www.mckendree.edu/academics/scholars/issue18/fremder.htm, accessed 20 June 2021

28 Baumeister, RF, Campbell, JD, Krueger, JI, and Vohs, KD, 'Does high self-esteem cause better performance, interpersonal success, happiness, or healthier lifestyles?', *Psychological Science in the Public Interest*, 4/1 (2003), 1–44, https://journals.sagepub.com/doi/10.1111/1529-1006.01431, accessed 20 April 2023

29 Seligman, MEP and Schulman, P, 'Explanatory style as a predictor of productivity and quitting among life insurance sales agents', *Journal of Personality and Social Psychology*, 50/4 (1986), 832–838, https://doi.org/10.1037/0022-3514.50.4.832, accessed 20 April 2023

The difference between male and female self-belief in the workplace may provide one explanation for the gender pay gap. In 2011, as part of a leadership and management survey, British managers were asked how confident they felt in their positions. Half of the female respondents reported having self-doubt about their job performance and career progression, compared to less than a third of male respondents.[30] This was echoed in the US three years later in an article entitled 'The confidence gap' by Katty Kay and Claire Shipman. The article suggests that because women are less self-assured than men, they come across as less successful and confident in the workplace and, as a result, don't get paid as much. They found that what you earn has as much to do with confidence as competence.[31]

So we know that having unshakeable belief in yourself will incrementally improve your life. I won't go as far as saying that all of life's big problems can be explained away by low self-confidence or a lack of self-belief, but I will say that the greatest antidote to dealing with the challenges of our times is having unshakeable self-belief.

How can we cultivate it – unshakeable self-belief?

30 'Ambition and gender at work', (Institute of Leadership & Management, 2011), www.institutelm.com/resourceLibrary/ambition-and-gender-at-work.html, accessed 20 April 2023.
31 Kay, K and Shipman, C, 'The confidence gap', (*The Atlantic*, May 2014), www.theatlantic.com/magazine/archive/2014/05/the-confidence-gap/359815, accessed 21 May 2022

Identifying boundaries and limiting beliefs

Before we can improve your self-belief, we must first identify the limiting beliefs that are standing in your way. One way to do this is to consider what you believe is possible in your life. Challenging your perceived limitations and boundaries is a powerful process that can lead to real shifts in awareness of your internal and external world. Challenging your existing beliefs is the first step to redesigning your belief system, which puts you in the position to actively choose, not passively accept, your beliefs.

WILD EXERCISE: Finding your boundary

Many people won't achieve their financial goals, not because they're incapable, but simply because they lose belief in themselves. This is a great exercise to illustrate this point.

I want you to write down how much money you'd like to make in the next 12 months. Now double it. Look at that number and pay attention to the first thought that comes into your mind. For example, you might want to make $100,000. When you double that, it's $200,000. If you feel like it's possible and you could make it happen, then consider if you believe you could earn $400,000 or $800,000 or even $1.6 million. You will reach a number where your brain hits the brakes and says, 'Oh, I don't think so.' That is the point of friction between what you believe is possible, with your relative time and resources, and what's outside the bounds of that possibility. It's an invisible ceiling and, once the average person hits it, they give up, because what's beyond it exceeds their perceived capabilities.

The ceiling marks your 'boundary conditions'. A boundary condition is a mental block, for example, a value, a belief or a gap in understanding, that holds you back and prevents you from growing beyond your current level of success in life. We'll go into more detail about that later when we discuss focus. The important point to understand now is the benefit of extending your boundaries. Oliver Wendell Holmes Sr, an American physician and poet, talked about the idea that 'a mind that is stretched by a new experience can never go back to its old dimensions'.[32] The beauty of this concept is that once you identify and work through your limiting beliefs, you'll never have to do it again because your mind has opened and is irreversibly changed. For example, think about learning to ride a bike. The skills required to ride a bike are completely different to the skills require to walk. When you try to balance on two wheels, your boundary condition, in this case the centre of gravity needed for walking, initially prevents you from finding your balance. With practice, you push the boundaries of your physiology to adapt your centre of gravity to balance on and successfully ride a bike. Once you have this skill, it's almost impossible to forget.

---

32 Holmes, OW, *The Autocrat of the Breakfast-Table*, (Phillips, Sampson, and Company, 1858), https://archive.org/details/autocratofbreakf00holm/page/n7/mode/2up, accessed 20 April 2023

As we discussed earlier, your beliefs are established in childhood during the imprint phase, and they come from the people closest to you. Therefore the simplest way of identifying limiting beliefs you might have is to observe the way your family talks about money, time, people, work, health and love. As the saying goes, you are the average of the people around you so these can provide clues about your limiting beliefs, which are often a reflection of the beliefs of your family and friends.

WILD EXERCISE: Identify limiting beliefs

Write down some of the main limiting beliefs that you think your family and friends have. Chances are, yours are similar. Some common limiting beliefs are:

- I'm not good enough
- I don't deserve success
- I fear failure
- I don't believe in myself
- I'm not worthy
- I won't/can't be loved
- I feel guilty about a past decision
- I'm not smart enough
- I'm not intelligent enough
- I'm too young/old
- I have anxiety and/or depression
- I don't have the ability to change

Many self-limiting beliefs centre around our individual perceived value. When we are feeling less than enough or undeserving of something, it is often a result of our comparison culture. If we get stuck in the comparison zone after too many hours scrolling social media, we tend to automatically overestimate the worth, skills and success of others and underestimate our own.

If we are feeling guilty about a decision we've made in the past, we are being held back by the belief that we should have done something differently. This guilt will eventually limit our ability to make any important decisions in the future, for fear of getting it wrong again.

When we feel we aren't smart enough to learn a new skill or are not intelligent enough to hold our own among our peers, we are being impacted by the captivity we were exposed to in the school system. The education system, for all its obvious merits, presents a limited number of successful paths forward within a single framework that is meant to be suitable for a multitude of learners. Beliefs around going to school, getting good grades and getting a job as the only pathway to success fall short when held up to the rigour of life.

Belief has also been shown to play a huge role in patient recovery. A study conducted on patients with Parkinson's disease showed that placebo treatment could induce the release of dopamine in the brain, improving the motor symptoms of the patients.[33]

---

33   Benedetti, F, Mayberg, HS, Wager, TD, Stohler, CS, and Zubieta, JK, 'Neurobiological mechanisms of the placebo effect', *The Journal of Neuroscience*, 25/45 (2005), 10390–10402, www.jneurosci.org/content/25/45/10390, accessed 26 April 2023

The belief in the treatment prompted improvements in the patients, even without the presence of actual medication.

WILD EXERCISE: The cost of your limiting beliefs

Now that we understand limiting beliefs and you have identified some of your own, I want you to consider the WILD cost of those beliefs. Look at the WILD Areas (wellness, income, love, lifestyle and direction) and categorise your most negative and limiting beliefs, using the table below.

As you do that, consider:

- What has been the cost in the short term and the long term?
- What have you lost over the past couple of years in the WILD Areas? (Wellness, Income, Love, Lifestyle and Direction).

Limiting belief eg I don't have time	Wellness	Income	Love/ Lifestyle	Direction
Short-term cost				
Long-term cost				

Cultivating unshakeable self-belief

Having identified your limiting beliefs and the costs they incur, you will no doubt be eager to cultivate unshakeable self-belief. To help you do this, I'm going to equip you with two survival skills you can use on the path toward your WILD life.

WILD EXERCISE: The power 100

The first survival skill I want to teach you will become a weapon against the limiting beliefs you encounter. It's called a Power 100 list. Like the space below, create a list or table of 100 achievements, accomplishments, creations, learnings, discoveries or explorations of which you're proud.

I know it's a daunting number – that is part of the power of the Power 100. List big things and small things. Consider that you didn't always know how to read, write, speak, walk, talk, tie your shoelaces or drive a car. Of course, you'll revel in listing the big accomplishments like graduating university, starting your own business, making your first sale, falling in love, getting married, having children and so on. Do not stop until you get to 100.

Your mind will hit a threshold but, if you persist, you'll go to another level.

Self-belief is built on the accumulation of small, repeated experiences. You don't have to wait for new experiences; you can build by going back through your memories. Doing this will arm you with a quiver full of self-esteem and self-confidence arrows to take with you on your journey into the wild. When you have moments of doubt, when you feel like you're lost, when you're under threat from the blocks and barriers of your past, you let loose an arrow. You have this artillery, this list of 100 things that you've done, which provides you with unshakeable self-belief in the face of any challenge you may encounter.

A new paradigm

The second survival skill is the ability to shift your limiting belief and replace it with a new paradigm. If you're going to enter the wild, then you need to make sure you take the right tools. We need to make sure we've packed our bags well and must operate from a new paradigm because the laws of the wild are very different from the laws of captivity.

WILD EXERCISE: New beliefs

Use the template below to identify the single biggest limiting belief holding you back.

When you think about the belief:

- What internal dialogue plays in your mind?
- What flashback images, memories or movies do you see?
- What sounds are significant? Eg people talking, shouting, laughing?
- How does that belief feel to think about? And where does the feeling live in your body?

Now think about a positive, empowered belief:

- What's something positive and uplifting that you believe about yourself?

Answer the same questions above for this positive and empowered belief, using the following template:

Negative/Limiting Belief:	Positive/Empowering Belief:
Images, Movies and Flashbacks:	Images, Movies and Flashbacks:
-	-
-	-
-	-
Sounds:	Sounds:
-	-
-	-
-	-

Negative/Limiting Belief:	Positive/Empowering Belief:
Feelings:	Feelings:
-	-
-	-
-	-
Inner Dialogue:	Inner Dialogue:
'_____'	'_____'

When you look at both lists, what do you notice? Try to look beyond the obvious 'good' or 'bad' aspects of these memories and feelings to how different the two experiences are. It's not the memory alone but the collection of images, sounds, feelings and negative dialogue around it that creates your limiting belief.

Before we can change a limiting belief, we need to have awareness of the building blocks of that belief. As you can see above, each belief is uniquely constructed and, if we can learn to manipulate these distinctions, we can regain control of our internal experience and change our beliefs almost instantly (well, within fifteen minutes).

The laws of the wild state that you are in complete control of your emotional, physical and financial freedom. As a result, we need to learn how to change limiting beliefs. The first step toward that change is learning how to map a limiting belief. This is a process we teach during our live programmes, and you can watch a belief transformation at www.wildsuccess.global/book. You'll see me complete a belief transformation in fifteen minutes with a client named Eleanor, who came to us looking for help to transform her limiting beliefs. If you come to one of our seminars, we'll show you how to change your mindset using neuroscience and, in a matter of minutes, shift limiting beliefs for life. If you can't get to an event, here are the steps to get clear on your limiting beliefs and then change them.

1. Identify the limiting belief (eg 'I'm not enough').

2. Map that limiting belief. Understand the distinctions, what we would refer to in neuroscience as the belief blueprint (eg visual, auditory, kinaesthetic, auditory, digital).

3. Now you need to create leverage. You need a compelling reason to release this belief. The belief exists for a reason and, at some level, it serves you. Consider the costs we talked about regarding wellness, income, love, lifestyle and direction.

4. Disrupt the limiting belief by considering it in different ways. Test the belief's validity – do you have any evidence in your life to suggest this belief is fiction and not fact? Consider that there may be another side to the coin; maybe there's a distinction that you haven't fully understood. List all the examples in your life where this belief has been proven wrong, all the people you know who have probably thought this same thing and still found a way to win. As you disrupt the limiting belief, you'll realise it doesn't have as

much hold over you. You start to develop tools such as the Power 100 list, which allow you to challenge the limiting belief.

5. Create a new, empowered belief. Ideally, this is the opposite of the old belief you've just worked through. Then, find evidence that reinforces the new belief and condition, condition, condition. What's important here is that you repeat and reaffirm this process daily until you've changed the belief.

Let's explore some of the positive beliefs that could change your life.

'I'm a work in progress'

When we experience difficult times, we tend to put unreasonable expectations on ourselves to be a finished product. But we're not. Adults are bad at learning new skills because we're used to being good at the things we can already do. We avoid taking risks because we have a perfectionism identity, which requires everything to be perfect all the time. If you embrace the belief, 'I'm a work in progress,' then failures and mistakes along the way won't affect you as much. You have given yourself permission to make mistakes, to still be in development. This belief makes difficult times easier because you don't expect yourself to be perfect, so you're okay with it when you're not. During the good times, this belief provides positive reinforcement. When you're doing great and still holding the belief, 'I'm a work in progress,' you are able to think, 'Wow, look what I've accomplished – imagine what else I can do.'

Under new management

In the same way that organisations can restructure, you can decide to vote in a new CEO or management team to run your life. If you've had experiences where things haven't worked, where you've tried to set goals and failed, where you've taken a step forward and then two or three steps back, this perspective shift allows you to embrace new ideas, beliefs and routines. An internal restructure allows you to accept that the old leadership and strategy are no longer effective and no longer allowed to hold you back. You can be clear about the fact that you're showing up, keeping yourself accountable and doing the best you can.

'If it's meant for me, it won't go past me'

This is a beautiful Scottish saying, which I interpret to mean that if you're doing your best, you shouldn't be concerned about how quickly you're moving, only with how fully you're showing up. Don't get me wrong, I want you to relentlessly pursue your goals. I also want you to be effective in that pursuit. If you find yourself coming up against red flag after obstacle after brick wall, and your progress toward that specific goal is going nowhere, you can give yourself permission to move on to the next one. That door just might not have been yours to open. This also allows for the belief that your past doesn't have to equal your future, and the rest of your life can be the best of your life. The next goal you chase is likely to put you in front of the door that will open.

'Anything is possible if I know how'

If I don't think something is possible, it's simply that I don't know how to do it yet. This belief puts me in a position of being consciously and constantly curious. I'm always searching for people and programmes that I can learn from and that can take my life to the next level. Finding a guide or a mentor is crucial to strengthening this belief. Take inspiration from someone with experience, who can challenge your limiting beliefs and show you the potential that you don't yet know you have.

Interview: Travis Jones

Travis Jones is a world-leading personal trainer, serial entrepreneur, mentor and coach. Back in 2014, when I first met TJ and his wife, Liv, they generously shared their wisdom with me to help me grow WILD Success, enabling me to change more lives. Within six months of our café meeting in South Melbourne,

WILD became a million-dollar business, expanded globally and the rest is history.

Travis and Liv built the hugely successful gym franchise, Result Based Training, and over a decade grew the group to twenty locations, with more than $10 million in annual revenue. They've started and built successful companies in marketing, supplements, business coaching and Pilates around the world. Today, Travis runs 'Fit Dads Club', a hugely popular coaching programme for dads who want to lose weight and have more energy for the thing that matters most – their family. They are dear friends and mentors to me. Without TJ and Liv, there would be no WILD Success. For this book, I sat down and spoke with Travis about the role self-belief has played in their success.

Calvin: What have been the biggest challenges you've dealt with in the past two years, personally and professionally?

Travis: This list could go on forever as the past two years in any business have been tough. I'm not one to dwell on the past or the challenges but we often have to reflect on these to see how we could have performed better. This is how we learn and how we grow. For me, the greatest challenge of COVID-19 was dealing with how the pandemic impacted the health and fitness space. Motivating staff when they weren't allowed to leave their house was central to that. Our staff gain significance and connection from being there in person, connecting with our clients and getting praise back from them for the job that they're doing; in this new reality, they had to entirely change the way they worked.

People were broken down because they didn't have certainty. They weren't certain in their job. They weren't certain in their growth. They weren't certain in moving forward with our business. We weren't told how long we were going to be locked down in our houses or how long our businesses were going to be closed. Constantly battling with that level of uncertainty, in a certainty-driven industry, was extremely tough. I was constantly challenged in my ability to keep people's vibrations high and their focus on gratitude.

We ended up closing our locations. We had some partnership issues. We've dealt with it all. I believe that life happens for you, not to you. No matter what issues we were facing, they were put there to provide us with the opportunity to grow. They were there to help us challenge ourselves to become better human beings. They were there as a catalyst to move us into the next phase of our lives. I do have the unshakeable self-belief that I'm here on this earth to change lives and, while my avenue for achievement may have shifted, that doesn't mean my end goal has.

Calvin: What limiting beliefs of the past did you have to release to survive and thrive in your life and business?

Travis: The limiting belief I released was being defined by my material wealth, by the things I thought I wanted. Looking back a couple of years, I believed I needed to have a certain car, a certain house, a certain lifestyle that would allow everyone else to accurately judge my success. I was bending under societal pressure and conforming to society's standard of success, when I needed to return to my core values and what I believe success to mean. I think success is an ever-changing landscape for us as humans. As we move through the different phases of our life, our definition of success changes. If you aren't changing your definition of success as you move forward through your life, you'll end up feeling stuck and unfulfilled. If your definition of success is tied to a monetary value, you'll constantly be unfulfilled. You can push and strive but, when you achieve your goal, this fleeting positive emotion lasts for a moment and then you need to reach another monetary value to feel successful again. In reality, success for me is being the best dad and the best husband I can be. It's a constant and never-ending journey of growth.

Calvin: What are your core beliefs and how have they helped you navigate this time?

Travis: My core beliefs are:

A sense of urgency – I have a sense of power, that I control my destiny on this earth.

Courage – I have the courage, in the face of uncertain times, to lean into resistance, to know that I back myself. If I have myself, my wife and my kids, I can lean into the resistance and push through any obstacle.

Perseverance – I understand that nothing lasts forever. The bad times don't last forever, but neither do the good times.

Passion – finding that love for what I do and the joy I feel when I wake up every single morning and do that thing I love.

Hope – the caveat with hope is you have to be doing the work but hope is knowing that tomorrow can be better than today. If I understand that life happens for me and not to me, I can keep doing the work. I can find the good and maintain perspective and gratitude.

Integrity – my word is my bond. The test of someone's character is not how they act in the best of times but how they act when the world is metaphorically burning around them.

Extreme ownership – you can make mistakes, but you have to own them. You have to own the part you play in everything you do because, if you can own it, you can move on from it. Failure is a necessity of growth – if you aren't willing to fail in life, you aren't going all-in. This is why it is so important to teach our children through the act of doing. Our kids don't listen to what we say, they listen to what we do. I must be a role model and example to them.

Calvin: How has mentorship helped you in your journey to challenge your beliefs and embrace new ways of thinking, personally and professionally?

Travis: I think mentoring can be so many different things. Mentoring can be found within your circle. You are the sum of the five people you spend the most time with. They lift you up in the values that they hold true and you can raise your vibration to reach their level. Conversely, discarding those people who don't lift you up is also a form of mentorship. Books are mentors. Through books, we gain knowledge that helps us move through trying times and understand that the world goes through cycles.

Whatever I'm going through, someone else has already gone through some version of that and made it through. And if they've done it, I can do it. And even if they didn't, I can learn from their mistakes and do it differently. Podcasts provide mentorship. They show us this common humanity, that you are not alone. And all of these resources make me believe in myself even more. They raise my thermostat of potential and lift me up. We are what we consume, and I consume things that raise me to be the person that I'm capable of being.

6
Emotional Mastery

Emotions are hugely varied and complicated. Given the complexity of our emotions, I think it is incredible that no one formally teaches us how to understand and interpret them. Emotions are something that we learn about through experience and, apart from maybe our parents, no one teaches us how to feel. When you're going through the primary, secondary and even university education systems (though think science and engineering, rather than arts and humanities), it's rare to have a teacher sit down and talk about emotions, how they're created and formed and the ability we have to change them. It's no wonder that during difficult, demanding times, we can find ourselves emotionally inept and unable to communicate effectively. We struggle with how to feel, think and process our emotions because no one ever showed us how or gave us the tools to work through these feelings. Most people think their emotions are a response to their environment, but science shows that in fact your environment and circumstances are responding to your emotions.[34] Your emotions are responsible for programming and shaping your environment.

How your emotions shape you

The English language has more than 3,000 words to describe emotions.[35] Incredibly, we rely on just six basic emotions on a daily basis; of those six, four are negative and two are positive.[36] Many people are travelling through their lives, unaware of their emotions until they are triggered by someone or something and they react emotionally. Most people are truly unaware of how they feel and what positive and negative triggers are in their lives. Consider keeping an emotional diary for even a few days and record hourly how you feel and what's happening in your life. Soon enough

34 Panksepp, J, 'Affective consciousness: Core emotional feelings in animals and humans', *Consciousness and Cognition*, 14/1 (2005), 30–80, http://doi.org/10.1016/j.concog.2004.10.004

35 Elert, E, '21 emotions for which there are no English words', (*Popular Science*, 2013), www.popsci.com/science/article/2013-01/emotions-which-there-are-no-english-words-infographic, accessed 21 May 2022

36 Cherry, K, 'The 6 types of basic emotions and their effect on human behaviour', (Very well Mind, 2021), www.verywellmind.com/an-overview-of-the-types-of-emotions-4163976, accessed 21 June 2021

you'll start to realise a pattern in your emotional life. One big shift in awareness many of my clients have had is in the generalisation of how they think they feel. Because the brain is constantly receiving and categorising information and stimuli, it takes the complexity of our emotional range and generalises the experience, putting several emotions together into one category.

I've often seen this first-hand with clients struggling with their mental health. When we have clients complete an emotional diary, we discover they feel a variety of emotions on a moment-to-moment basis, such as feeling melancholy or bitter, lethargic or heartbroken, irritable or annoyed. When they review this list at the end of the day, because their overall experience is negative, they'll often label how they feel as being in a 'state of depression'. This generalisation of emotions can prevent people from shifting depression, because placing multiple and varied feelings into one category of 'depression' can magnify the problem and create a negative cycle. A 2018 study found talking about feelings, writing about them, or simply picking a feeling after reviewing a list instantly reduced people's distress. 'Naming feelings decreased the duration and intensity of uncomfortable emotions.'[37]

---

37 Torre, JB and Lieberman, MD, 'Putting feelings into words: Affect labeling as implicit emotion regulation', *Emotion Review*, 10/2 (2018), 116–124, https://doi:10.1177/1754073917742706

Our emotional state directly impacts our overall results. Let's look at how our emotions could impact an attempt at weight loss. Consider this cycle of weight loss results: you start off and get a bad result (you didn't lose any weight) or you don't get the result you wanted (you lost only one kilo instead of three), which stirs up a variety of emotions like frustration, anger, incompetence and defeat. As a result, you tend to fester in that emotional space ('I can't lose weight'), which prevents you from working to create a more positive emotional space ('I lost a kilo – it's a small step in the right direction'). This emotional state will then also reinforce negative beliefs ('I've tried every diet and I just can't lose weight').

Now consider the alternative. If you're feeling pretty good ('I didn't expect to lose any weight but I shifted a kilo'), then you're more likely to take positive actions ('I'm going to keep making healthier food choices') and, as a result, find yourself feeling fantastic and taking even greater actions ('I felt so good avoiding processed food today, I'm going to take a walk in the sunshine now'), which means you're going to get equally great results ('Wow, I made two small changes and I've lost three kilos'). This will reinforce unshakeable self-belief ('I am capable of taking control of my choices and getting positive outcomes'). Seeing these two opposite pathways and outcomes, how would you choose to manage your emotions? I know I would much prefer to feel positive, do great things and get great results. The key is being aware of what you're feeling and why so that you can be in control of your emotions, not the other way around.

Why owning your emotions matters

In certain conversations, more than 90% of our communication can be nonverbal,[38] making it all about energy and emotion. It also means a lot of what happens occurs via autopilot reactions. The following two examples illustrate how deeply we can be affected by what we feel subconsciously.

A Yale University study focused on the emotional reactions people have toward seemingly trivial life experiences.[39] The research involved hot and cold cups of coffee. On a city street, trained actors would reach out to somebody and say, 'Excuse me, would you mind just holding my coffee?' Then they handed the participant a coffee cup and reached down to tie their shoelaces. Half of the participants held a hot coffee and the others held a cold coffee. About twenty minutes later, researchers would catch up with those people and say, 'Hey, we'll pay you $20 if you would just complete a short survey.' In the survey, they were asked to read a short character description from a novel and then describe the character's traits and mannerisms by choosing from a list of options.

The participants read the same paragraph and interacted with the same actors. The only difference was that one group had held a hot cup of coffee and the other a cold cup of coffee. The results were astonishing.

---

38 Mehrabian, A, *Nonverbal Communication* (New Brunswick: Aldine Transaction, 1972)

39 'With hot coffee, we see a warm heart, Yale researchers find', (Yale News, 2008), https://news.yale.edu/2008/10/23/hot-coffee-we-see-warm-heart-yale-researchers-find, accessed 17 May 2022

The study reported that 80% of the people who held a hot cup found the character in the story to be warm, tolerant, accepting and loving. Conversely, 81% of people who held a cold cup found the same character to be cold, distant and with a negative demeanour. The only difference was the temperature of the cup. If a hot or cold coffee cup can impact your perception to that extent, imagine how all the stimuli we receive throughout the day, whether face to face or through the different types of media we are exposed to, affect how we feel – and we don't even realise it.

Another example that demonstrates how our daily habits and experiences shape our emotional landscape comes from a University of Queensland study conducted over ten years with a group of 9,000 women.[40] Researchers looked at two different groups of women. One group had a job that required they sat for less than seven hours a day and they did zero physical activity; the second group sat for four or more hours per day and they did the recommended amount of physical activity. The results showed that the amount of time spent sitting didn't impact the likelihood of depression; however, the group of women who did zero physical activity were three times more likely to develop symptoms of depression.

That's a substantial difference. I'm not going to go into depth about why exercising is good, other than

40   van Uffelen, JG, van Gellecum, YR, Burton, NW, Peeters, G, Heesch, KC, and Brown, WJ, 'Sitting-time, physical activity, and depressive symptoms in mid-aged women', *American Journal of Preventive Medicine*, 45/3 (2013), 276–81, https://doi.org.10.1016/j.amepre.2013.04.009

to say that it has massive physiological, psychological and emotional benefits. Even low-impact exercise like walking is enough to get those juices flowing and, as proven by the above study, it's essential for good mental health

It is so important to be aware and proactive when it comes to your emotions. The coffee cup example shows how a small detail in our day, something we probably wouldn't even remember, can be the difference between a positive or negative emotional response. The research on exercise proves that taking control of your environment, and how you act within it, can have a huge impact on your emotional outcomes and your overall wellbeing. Both examples probably make you wish you had learned how to bring awareness to your emotions sooner – don't wait another minute.

Identifying your emotions

How do we become aware of the emotions that hold us back and how do we identify the parts of our daily lives that trigger negative emotions? The first step is to bring awareness to your emotional state. My favourite way of doing that is by journaling the emotions I feel throughout the day.

WILD EXERCISE: Emotional triggers

Write down ten emotions, both positive and negative, that you've experienced today. For example, you may have experienced negative emotions of anger, apprehension, anxiety, fear and fatigue, and positive emotions such as gratitude, excitement, joy, wonder and amusement.

With your list in front of you, can you identify some triggers for each of those emotions? What happened in that moment? What specific action made you feel a certain way? Because we all have varying levels of awareness around our emotions, this task will take more practice and patience if you tend to race through your day unaware of how you're feeling and why. If that sounds like you, stop reading right now and write down the first emotion that comes to mind, then write down the trigger. That's your first practice complete. Let me give you an example of some of the feelings I've experienced recently and their triggers:

Emotion	Trigger
Love	Listening to our wedding song, 'Higher Love' (the cover version by Whitney Houston).
Freedom	Waking up in a new city and walking the streets.
Purpose	Working with a client at a seminar and seeing their life transformed when they learn a new skill.
Frustration	Waiting in line behind someone who is taking a long time to decide.

Now that you have an awareness of your emotions, I want you to identify which, both positive and negative, are frequently occurring – in other words, those that have become habitual. If you want to change anything you do in your life, you must first change how you feel about it. Looking at your list, there are three different ways you can approach emotions and triggers. The first is to develop a high level of awareness around common experiences that trigger certain emotions for you. The goal is to avoid negative triggers and do your best to engage with positive triggers. For example, I know certain foods are going to make me feel great and others are going to make me feel unhealthy. If I want to avoid feelings of regret or disappointment, I know to pick the healthy option and stay away from the sugary or fatty indulgences that don't make me feel good.

Additionally, we can look at our emotions and triggers as tools to help us rewire our brains in a positive way. Then we are no longer resigned to being controlled by the negative experiences. Fundamentally, emotional mastery comes down to one thing: you need to learn how to use emotions and not let emotions use you.

If you have a high level of emotional awareness, you might be able to identify the triggers before they occur and work to eliminate them from your life. Try to think about a negative emotion that you feel regularly, maybe frustration. For example, you find yourself regularly feeling extremely frustrated when you're driving. You're frustrated at the red light.

Frustrated with the person who's not driving at the speed limit. Frustrated with the person who cut you off. Now ask yourself, 'Why am I repeating this "same stuff, different day" cycle?' The answer is likely that you're letting your emotions run unchecked and this experience is now a habit-enforced behaviour. Now ask yourself, 'When do I feel like this?' Imagine that experience again. Rewind the tape and look closely at what was happening. Who was there? Were you alone, with your parents, your partner or a friend? What were the circumstances? Were you in a hurry – were you on your way to work or the gym? Try to identify the small distinctions that made the difference.

While thinking about triggers, it's also helpful to question who you learned this emotion from. You weren't born this way. You've developed this emotional response over time by observing human behaviour around you. I understood the power of emotions early on. Even as a young boy, I could grasp how difficult they were to master. I grew up in a loving and caring family, which was (like most families) also flawed. My father is a passionate and intense man, like his father before him. When triggered, Dad's intensity and passion would quickly become frustration and he'd often lose his temper in a flash of rage and anger. Looking back now, I know he simply had never developed the skills to manage his intensity and channel it into something more positive; he allowed his emotions to control him. While he was never physically violent, I remember him flying off the handle and losing his temper. As a young man, I began to copy the emotions and responses I saw him 'model' and, before long, found myself with an anger issue. I'll never forget the day my mother said, 'You're not going to be like your father,' and took me to see a specialist who practised something that I now know as the 'emotional freedom' technique. After just one session, I was able to release the anger that I was unconsciously holding. I wasn't an angry kid; I was simply acting out the response I had learned from my environment. Today, I'm proud to say that I don't have an anger issue. Sure, I feel anger like anyone else, but I don't allow my anger to take over.

You live your life from wherever you are emotionally. These habitual emotions have a bigger impact than you realise because of the way our emotions shape the world around us. Our lives are full of obstacles and challenges, any one of which can reach crisis level. Luckily, you can learn to master your emotions. By proactively conditioning yourself, you can be successful in managing your emotional reactions to those daily crises.

Paradigm shift: emotions are skills

Can you identify some core emotions you consistently express? As emotional creatures, we often tend to associate our personality, and therefore our identity, with our emotions. Consider the friend who's always the centre of attention, who might be extraverted, confident or charismatic, and equally the friend who's more reserved – they can both be labelled anxious, cautious or even shy. People use language to further reinforce these emotions and link them with their identity. For example, compare 'I'm an anxious person' with 'I am skilled at feeling anxious'. Thinking about our emotions as skills allows us to rationalise that *we* are not anxious, rather, we have learned the skill of anxiety and now we're good at 'doing' anxiety because we've seen and practised it a lot. This mindset allows you to distance yourself from the experience of anxiety, meaning you're more in control, more likely to look at the emotion objectively and more likely to be able to change it.

This concept of emotions being skills is one of the biggest breakthroughs in positive psychology. Embracing the notion that we sit on a spectrum of emotional competence is incredibly empowering. It puts control back in your hands. Whatever you practise you'll get better at, so if you invest the time to learn how to be more courageous, kind and compassionate you will learn to master those skills like Beethoven mastered the piano.

Personally, I want to learn how to become more patient, tolerant and accepting of others. I want to learn how to be more generous, grateful and loving toward others. I don't want to learn more about how to be sad or anxious; I want less of those things. It follows that I choose to avoid situations, or limit the time I spend with people, that cause me to experience or *practise the skills* of sadness and anxiety. When we look at the differences between successful and unsuccessful people, we often see a separation of emotional skills, such as tenacity, courage, perseverance, dedication, resourcefulness and determination from those of doubt, worry, scepticism and fear.

As a young man I realised I didn't always embody the emotions I saw in successful people, so I became obsessed with understanding how I could learn and then master them. I don't believe in the concept of 'fake it 'til you make it', Instead I always thought of growing emotionally as 'working on it until you own it'.

The exercise below will help you identify the costs of not mastering your emotions.

WILD EXERCISE: The cost of negative emotions

Identify the most limiting, negative emotion that holds you back in the areas of wellness, income, love, lifestyle and direction, and think about what it has cost you.

As you do that, consider:

- What has been the cost in the short term and the long term?
- What have you lost over the past couple of years in the WILD Areas?

Negative emotion eg self-doubt	Wellness	Income	Love/ Lifestyle	Direction
Short-term cost				
Long-term cost				

Cultivating emotional mastery

I'm a huge sports fan and I'm very competitive. I've been obsessed with winning for as long as I can remember. For this reason, even though I'm Australian, I've always been a fan of the New Zealand All Blacks rugby team, who are among the most successful sporting teams of all time. I had the pleasure of working with Gilbert Enoka, the peak performance coach for the All Blacks, who has led them to back-to-back world championships on two separate occasions. I asked him, 'What are the differences that made the difference? Why are the All Blacks so successful?'

He told me that there have been two things in the past hundred years that have stayed the same for the New Zealand All Blacks. One is the silver fern that they wear on their crest and the other is the haka. Now, no doubt you've seen the haka. If you haven't, please watch it on YouTube. The haka is a powerful warrior ritual that has been around for millennia, designed to prepare the Maori people for gruesome battles ahead. The words of some hakas translate to: 'You die, you die. We live, we live.' Can you imagine standing on the rugby pitch, with a group of All Blacks staring back at you intensely while performing an aggressive haka and shouting at you that you're going to die and they're going to live? It certainly elicits a strong emotional reaction.

The haka, because of its effectiveness as an emotional primer, is something we have modelled and incorporated into our work. We don't teach people how to do the haka but we do teach people to execute what's known as a 'precision anchor'. A precision anchor is any event or action that is linked to a strong emotional response, either positive or negative. Precision anchors are created automatically by the external stimulus we receive through touch, sights, sounds, smells or tastes. For example, a lot of people will remember exactly where they were on 9/11, the day the Twin Towers collapsed. The day stands out because it is linked to a strong emotional response to what people saw, heard and felt when they got the news. That event left a lasting impression in people's minds in the same way that your wedding song, the moment of your child's birth or your first kiss leaves a substantial lasting memory.

In psychology this is known as 'stimulus response', a term that was coined by psychologist Ivan Pavlov.[41] When Pavlov began researching stimulus response, which we now refer to as precision anchoring, he discovered that dogs would salivate before they were going to be fed and realised he could stimulate the salivation response using a trigger of his choosing. He completed a series of studies in which he would ring a bell and then feed the dogs, until the dogs learned to associate the ringing of the bell with the delivery of food. After some time, even if no food was presented, the dogs would salivate upon receiving the aural stimulus of the ringing bell. We are (usually) more

---

41 Pavlov, IP, *Conditioned Reflexes: An investigation of the physiological activity of the cerebral cortex*, (Oxford University Press, 1927), https://archive.org/details/conditionedrefle00pavl, accessed 20 April 2023

intelligent than our canine counterparts but the work of Pavlov is still relevant today. Marketers understand this effect well, which is why we have jingles, logos and scents associated with big companies and fast-food chains, to ignite our collective desire for, or salivation over, their products.

Using this theory, we can see everything in life as a stimulus designed to trigger an emotional response. The clothes we wear, the food we eat, the cars we drive, where we work, what we do in our spare time and what we focus our time, energy and money on all trigger certain emotional responses. We are living our emotional lives through the things we do, see, hear, feel and touch. When we realise this about the world around us, we are empowered to more effectively control our emotions. By taking control, you can program your environment to trigger the emotions you want to feel. If you want to feel more confident, then create triggers or precision anchors that inspire feelings of confidence. If you want to feel more loved, generous, appreciated or connected, then you need to design your responses accordingly to stimulate the feeling you want. This is not wishful thinking; it is the science of precision anchoring.

Successful emotional mastery begins with an understanding that nothing in your life has meaning except the meaning you give it. Let me explain this with another anecdote about my grandparents. Earlier I mentioned the impact my grandparents had on my belief system. You'll remember that my gran, Elizabeth, is the spiritual one; her husband, my grandad, James Brian, was the furthest from spiritual that you can imagine. Grandad Brian passed away from cancer when I was a teenager. I'll never forget heading back to the UK for his funeral (my first trip to the UK since we left in '94) and seeing the pain of the loss my dad and gran were feeling.

About a year later, I was working at the local cinema, selling popcorn and lollies, when weird coincidences started happening. Have you ever looked at the clock and noticed matching numbers and patterns, like 11.11 or 13.13 or 3.33? This started happening to me. All. The. Time. I start to notice it so often that it gets a bit scary. At one point, I felt like Neo in *The Matrix*. Everywhere I looked, I was seeing numbers and patterns in random things. I'll never forget 5 January 2007, when it got so bad, I was getting concerned for my mental health. I honestly thought something was broken in my head. I mentioned it to my dad's partner and she asked me when it had started and if there were any days where it was particularly bad. 'Yes,' I replied emphatically. 'It started in November and yesterday it was intense.' She pointed out that the anniversary of Grandad Brian's passing was 18 November and that 5 January had been his birthday. She suggested that maybe he was trying to communicate with me.

I was blown away. All this time, Grandad was trying to communicate with me and I had been missing the signs. After that, I started paying closer attention and I found that, more often than not, when I was feeling emotionally triggered or mentally reaching out for guidance, I would look at the clock and what time would I see? 11.11 or 1.11 or 13.13. I would immediately be able to find calm and get back to my centre. Those times became messages of support and guidance from Grandad and those numbers have now become a positive anchor in my life. When I feel untethered or like I'm going off track, I'll look to the clock. I'll see the time and I can come back to myself. It might sound strange, but it works for me.

Everything and anything in your life can become an anchor for positive emotions. When you learn how to identify and create anchors, you set yourself up for success; you're programming your brain and your nervous system to create positive associations. This works in the same way as the hot cup of coffee from the Yale study producing a more positive response. It's one thing to be handed a hot cup of coffee, but this practice is even more important for the times that you're stuck holding the cold cup. You're always going to have conflict or friction points in your day. The key is finding the positive anchors that help you manage and recover from those tough patches.

WILD EXERCISE: Power emotions

This exercise expands upon the emotional triggers exercise you completed earlier, but this time you're actively choosing the emotions you want to feel and designing the triggers that will bring them to life.

You can't do the work of mastering your emotions if you don't identify them first. To better understand your emotions and triggers, set an hourly alarm for the next eight hours of your day, every day for the next week.

Every hour on the hour while you're awake, when the alarm sounds, get out your journal and identify how you feel in that moment and why (look past the annoyance of the alarm to identify another emotion). What we're looking to identify are your commonly experienced emotions and what triggers them. What you're looking to accomplish next is to become master of your emotions.

The most important question to consider is: how do you want to respond? Once you create an awareness of your emotional triggers, you're in a better position to choose the emotional response to those triggers. You choose to be conscious rather than unconscious about how you're feeling and acting. This will require that you change the way you think about your emotions. I'm challenging you to stop making excuses such as, 'I can't help the way I feel,' or 'There's nothing I can do, my emotions got the better of me.'

Write down your five power emotions and the triggers you want to activate those desired emotions.

List five emotions you would like to feel	What triggers could you create?
1.	1.
2.	2.
3.	3.
4.	4.
5.	5.

You can design a variety of anchors and rituals. They might include memories, songs, images, objects, affirmations, movements, videos, playlists and vision boards. Any of these things can become anchor points for you in your life.

Below is a list of some positive anchors I've created in my life that have been enormously effective in cultivating positive emotions.

Anchor	Emotion
Photo of Ash and Alila on my phone	Love, joy, purpose and connection
Renting houses/staying in hotels with epic views	Feelings of expansion, possibility and motivation
Reading/listening to audiobooks every week	Growth, progress and development
Memento mori (reminder of the inevitability of death) poster in my office	Reminds me how long (or not) I have left to live and creates a sense of urgency in going after my dreams
Event playlist	Playing the WILD event playlists in the office between events creates an energy similar to the live events to inspire and motivate the team

You can download an emotional mastery audio file at www.WILDSuccess.global/book where I take you through the process of installing five power emotions into your life in a matter of minutes.

The wild paradigm I want you to embrace is this: 'I can have total control over my emotions.' In any given situation, how you feel accounts for 10% of the outcome, the other 90% is how you choose to react.

The challenge is to make sure you use the emotions and don't let the emotions use you. When negative things happen, use that energy, use that drive, use that frustration, anger or determination and choose to be productive instead of destructive. Remember, awareness precedes change. You can't change an emotional range until you're aware of what's going on. This is not something that happens overnight. Since we already know how unconscious emotions can be, it is helpful to remind yourself that they are skills that you can work on until you own them. The crucial first step is to identify the trigger points for negative emotions and increase the gap between triggering and reacting. This awareness will allow you to choose, while in that gap, how you will react.

Once we decide on the new emotional responses we want to embrace, we need to condition, condition, condition those new emotions until they become second nature. For example, if you want to condition the experience of self-confidence, you have to choose to be confident every day and in every experience. From a practical perspective, that could involve setting a desktop screensaver to visually trigger the feeling of confidence. It could also involve designing a playlist that will trigger the same feeling (perhaps including the self-mastery audio file mentioned above) or carrying a photo that causes you to reflect on an achievement you are proud of. By default, this conditioning also includes removing yourself from situations or avoiding people that make you feel uncomfortable or lacking in confidence.

When I was at university, I represented Australia at the ENACTUS World Cup (an international social entrepreneurship competition). After my presentation, I received the feedback that my style was too polished and corporate, which caused my message to lack the heart and connection required to have the desired impact on the audience. To correct this, I hit on an unusual idea. I had one of my team members sit in the front row of the audience holding up a birthday card I'd received from my baby brother. As I was presenting and looking around the room, I would see the card and be reminded of him. Turning my thoughts to my beloved brother helped me soften my tone and speak from the heart while I was presenting. It was a simple visual trigger that allowed me to access the emotion needed to better connect with my audience and deliver my message with heart and warmth.

Ask yourself: 'How would the best version of me show up in a moment like this?' Then think about what emotions are required to create that version of you. You can go back to the power emotions exercise to find the answers as these moments arise.

Interview: Casey O Anaru

At the start of her thirties, Casey was a single mum of three healthy, beautiful kids. She had secured a new job as a prison officer, bought her own house and was enjoying greater financial independence. With the big pieces in place, she was finally ready to work on herself, so she started healing, unpacking and redefining who she wanted to be. Around this time, she started an online business in personal branding and affiliate marketing that involved a lot of personal development work. She loved it; she was literally addicted to it – every waking moment was about learning something new, implementing strategies or improving life in some way.

Fast forward five years and Casey and her new partner had a beautiful two-month-old son. Just when everything seemed to be settling into place, she faced the biggest crisis of her life thus far – the news that their infant son had cancer. His new life was supposed to be exciting and full of possibility, so to then look into her baby's eyes, so innocent, so sweet and utterly reliant on her, Casey was heartbroken. Their lives had turned on a dime with this crushing news. In the interview below, I talk to Casey about how in the face of such hardship, she was able to master her emotions and channel her purpose.

Calvin: What does 'living a WILD life' mean to you?

Casey: Living a WILD life means living with integrity and in alignment – always. This means being who you truly are (no lying to yourself, no bullshit) and being totally unapologetic about doing what feels right for you, despite what anyone else thinks you 'should' do, 'should' believe or 'should' feel.

Calvin: When you find yourself in crisis, how do you attain or maintain control over your emotional reactions?

Casey: I would answer this with a question. Why are we here? Why are we on this earth? For what purpose? Everyone has some purpose and I believe this is key to understanding our emotional reactions. Personally, I believe that I am here to contribute to the collective human experience. Everything I do or believe has a direct impact on the experiences and interactions I have with others.

Before I came to know this, I have to admit I didn't manage my emotions well at all. My parents had completely different approaches to dealing with their emotions. My dad was outspoken, loud, aggressive and sometimes even dominating, while my mum was submissive and reserved, keeping all her thoughts and opinions to herself. Their conflicting styles were not a great foundation but their traits carried over into the way I expressed myself and reacted to situations in life. It was messy. I did things the hard way. When a crisis would arise, such as my experience of infidelity and the way that person diminished my feelings, I would initially get loud and angry, then I would go silent, retreat inward and hate on myself. I would replay the scene over and over until I plunged myself into dark places where I wished for life to end.

I couldn't have anticipated experiencing anything that hurt as much as what I had been through with my ex, until we got the news that our infant son had cancer. The initial blow knocked me for six. I was in such shock, I didn't know if what I had heard was real. I had so many questions. I had no idea what to do next. I had to face so many life changes in that single moment. But one thing I knew, one thing I had learned through all the personal development and spirituality work I had done, was that this was happening for a reason. Cliché, I know, but so damn true. Although I couldn't see it in that moment, it soon became apparent that, through my son's diagnosis, he/we would impact the lives of thousands of people and help raise thousands of dollars for the charities that supported us along the way. It seemed our journey was tied in with the lives of other, similarly impacted families.

In hindsight, I realised that everything I had gone through up to his diagnosis had been for the purpose of getting me and my family through this crisis. This taught me that the challenges we are given, great or small, are all opportunities to learn, to grow and to gain wisdom. What I think in every moment I am challenged is: 'What am I here to learn, what wisdom can I gain and who can I possibly help in the future?'

I take a breath, become the observer and study what I'm feeling in that moment to get to the root of where my feelings are coming from. I put aside my ego, step into my vulnerability and ask my higher self how I should respond. The answer is always, 'With love, compassion and understanding.' Anything other than that will end in disaster.

Calvin: How do you identify your emotional triggers and what is your recommendation to someone who is trying to improve how they react to their own?

Casey: I trust my gut. My intuition is my guide to knowing when something isn't right for me. I notice how my body is feeling, what my initial thoughts are and what my impulse reactions would potentially be. I ask myself, 'What just happened? What does this mean to me? And what am I going to do about it?' These questions help me 'get myself right' so I can act in alignment with my higher self. These are the tools I've developed through your programmes and mentoring.

I would tell anyone on the journey to identifying their triggers to be intentional and be willing to do the work. Find the resources to help you explore who you are and what gets your goat up. This could be in the form of self-help books, podcasts, a mentor, a coach or simply journaling.

Calvin: How did finding a mentor impact on your journey?

Casey: Having a mentor was one of the biggest game-changers in uncovering who I am, what I want and how to achieve my goals, dreams and desires. I always knew I wanted to run my own business but, without a degree or business background, I never thought it was something I could do. I thought working a traditional job, trading my time for money, was the only way to make a living. I also knew that I wanted to live a 'f*** yes' life; I wanted to achieve freedom, to be unrestricted by time and finances and have the ability to be with my family when I chose. Living my life on someone else's clock never sat well with me.

When I came across you and the incredible, life-changing work you're doing at WILD Success, I was over the moon. You helped me deep dive into who I was at my core. You taught me a specific skill set and range of tools I could share with others. But it was the business strategy that brought it all together. You showed me that I didn't need the degree. Through your programmes and mentorship, I found a new sense of self-belief and confidence that I desperately needed to dive into my coaching business.

7
Powerful Behaviours

Unshakeable self-belief and emotional mastery are the foundation of your internal alignment because they provide a profound understanding of who you are and why you are that way. We will now look at the final two aspects of internal alignment, the first of which is creating powerful behaviours. I believe that your habits, routines and rituals are important because they are the minute mechanisms of long-term success creation.

Why habits are so hard to change

What is a habit? It's a series of thoughts, ideas, actions, behaviours, emotions and mannerisms that we repeat consistently. How we function, whether efficiently or inefficiently, is the result of our habits. The big question is, why is it so difficult to change our habits? It is because, as the saying goes, we are creatures of habit. Just as we have integrated emotions and beliefs during our imprint phase, we have also developed habits while in that absorption mode. We are attempting to establish patterns within our library of stimuli, if you will, that we will recognise later in life. These patterns are crucial for differentiating friend from foe, safe from unsafe and success from defeat. Those same patterns enforce our habits, routines and rituals.

Habits are hard to change because they are created as a survival response. The habits you have today evolved to guarantee your survival. Consider this in relation to your eating habits. We have all had the experience of not feeling hungry but, on smelling or seeing food, autopilot takes over and we eat anyway. You know you're not hungry, the food might not even taste good, but you find yourself eating even though you had no real desire to. Why? It's because, after millennia of feast or famine, your brain has been programmed to see food as a scarce resource. Early humans would go days without food, so when they caught or found food, they would immediately eat, gorge and feast to prepare for the next period of famine. It's the reason that our bodies are adept at holding body fat – it's a survival mechanism, which makes getting in shape and staying in shape so much harder. That same mechanism is responsible for the habit of consumerist spending versus saving for long-term wealth. If your goal is to survive in the short term, then you're going to focus on getting what you want (or think you need) in the present moment. You're not thinking long term. Especially if you're feeling stressed and overwhelmed, you're not thinking about long-term survival or investing for generational wealth; you're just thinking about what's right in front of you. Our ancestors, over thousands of years, only thought as far ahead as their next meal. We have the luxury of planning for our grandchildren, even great-grandchildren, so we must consciously build and enforce the pathways in our brains to reinterpret these survival skills for our evolved worldview.

The pathways I'm referring to are made from cells called neurons. As Canadian psychologist Donald Hebb says, 'Neurons that fire together, wire together.'[42] When we participate in an activity or action requiring any kind of intensity, whether that be pain or pleasure, we are creating the blueprint for that action to become a behaviour, routine or ritual. You can do something once and that's a behaviour; do it consistently and that's a routine; do it *automatically* and it has become a ritual.

Consider brushing your teeth. Initially, you will have had to rely on a lot of external stimulation from your parents telling you to brush your teeth. Over time, you will have started brushing your teeth independently. Now, you never leave the house without brushing your teeth. You don't want to deal with the social consequences of having bad breath and you are

---

42 Hebb, DO, *Organization of Behaviour: A neuropsychological theory* (Wiley, 1949)

so accustomed to the feeling of clean teeth that the feeling has become your preference. This process has gone from a behaviour that you learned, to a habit that you engrained, to a ritual that you must do before moving on to anything else.

Identifying your habits

Before I go any further, I want you to take a moment and think about your current routines and rituals. If I were to follow you for the day, what actions would I notice you taking consistently? Beyond human necessities and personal hygiene, what are some of the unique habits you've done for so long, you forget you do them? If you can bring awareness to your habits and identify those that are preventing you from living a WILD life, you can start to create change.

WILD EXERCISE: Becoming aware of behaviours

A simple way to bring awareness to your behaviours is to imagine you're charting two lines, one green and one red, both with arrows at the end (see figure below). Positive actions that align with your goals and dreams will take the green line in an upward trajectory, indicating that you are achieving what you desire from your life. Conversely, if you fail to take those actions or indulge in negative behaviours, you'll find yourself with a declining red line.

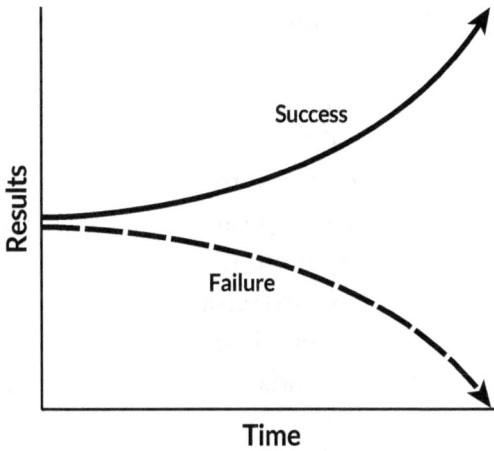

Now write down eight to ten rituals that you do each day and beside each item mark a red or a green dot. If you were to plot those dots as lines on the graph would the green line outpace the red? Behaviours that move the green line up take you in the direction of getting more of what you want in life and show that your actions and behaviours align with your goals and dreams. If you find yourself going further down the red line, you are moving away from your goals and dreams and might be crossing into self-sabotage.

If you consider the list you made for the above exercise, there will be two types of daily habits: those that are set in stone, for example, the morning coffee you simply cannot function without, and those that are a result of making a choice. This morning, I got up and I chose to go to the gym. I was late for my normal scheduled class, so I decided to just do weights instead. Although this was a change to my routine, it was better than skipping a workout session entirely. In that same situation, the old Calvin would've gone, 'Oh f***, I'm a couple minutes late for the gym. Let's not worry about it. I'll just train tomorrow.'

In that moment, I made the decision to stay on the green line, to enforce my positive habit of working out, as opposed to dropping to the red line and enforcing a negative habit of not exercising. Everything that you put into your body, every time you spend money, every time you create a calendar event, every thought you have about something, you are extending either the green line or the red line. This is why it is so important to build an awareness of the habits you already have.

I'll give you an incredible example of this. Like many people, I had connected celebrations with food and alcohol. As a child, if I did well in school or sport, we'd celebrate with takeaway or going out to a restaurant. As my business started to grow, I found myself celebrating too often and my health (and wallet) suffered. What compounded matters was travelling with work which limited my access to healthy food. Often our events and conferences would finish way after traditional food outlets had closed, leaving me with only unhealthy options for dinner. The more successful I became the worse the problem got. My success in the income and direction sectors of my life was having negative consequences in the wellness aspect of my life.

Nothing changed until I decided to hire my own personal trainer (now my wife) to help me set some new habits and routines that worked with my schedule. Ash had a completely different mindset to me in this area and revolutionised my health and fitness. We organised healthy meals before travel, made smoothies at events and when there were no other options, we'd either fast or choose the best options available. She showed me that it's possible to have it all, you just need to prepare and get organised.

The decisions we make reflect our habits, routines and rituals. They highlight our mindsets. They are influenced by what is referred to in NLP as 'meta programmes'. Meta programmes are the overarching models or habits a person repeats consistently that determine how they interact with the world.[43] For example, consider someone who has lost weight. That person has been successful because they were able to alter their meta programme, which transformed them from being someone with poor eating habits to someone with great eating habits. They shifted their previous model of being someone who did not prioritise exercise to someone who now has consistent training habits. Meta programmes don't just influence what we do, they also dictate what we don't do. If you consider a successful person, in any field or endeavour, their success is a function of their habits, routines and rituals. It can also be attributed to the habits they have broken or avoided creating, like snacking late at night or choosing to sit and watch six hours of Netflix instead of going for a walk after dinner and getting to sleep at a reasonable hour.

---

43   Hall, LM and Bodenhamer, BG, *Figuring Out People: Design engineering with meta-programs: deepening understanding of people for better rapport, relationships, and influence* (Crown House Publishing, 1997)

Think about anything that you desire in life, be it material things, success, more wealth, a better relationship, deeper spiritual connection or being able to live life on your own terms free from fear, worry and anxiety. All those things are determined by what you do on a daily basis. Your habits, routines and rituals, the things that you do repeatedly and perhaps unconsciously, determine if you fail or succeed. To paraphrase Aristotle, 'We are what we repeatedly do. Excellence then, is not an act, it is a habit.'[44]

Let's look at your finances. If you want to transform your finances, it's not about making more money, it's about creating better financial habits. The habits of saving, spending, investing and negotiating all become significant. I remember hearing a story about a gambler who had lost a huge amount of money. Someone had asked him, 'You had millions of dollars. How did you lose everything?' He replied, 'Well, it started slowly. And then, after a while, it all just fell apart.' This shows how you start with small losses and those small losses compound. The same goes for habits; if you start with a few bad habits, then more bad habits are easier to accept. It's important to acknowledge that habits and rituals are the bedrock of success and, without them, we can't possibly win long term. In business I always remind my clients of the rule of three, which states: once is a fluke, twice is a coincidence and three times is a trend. The goal is to create a *habit* of winning, not just to win.

---

44 Aristotle, Ross, WD, and Brown, L, *The Nicomachean Ethics* (Oxford University Press, 2009)

Cultivating powerful behaviours

If you can do something once, well done, but that doesn't mean you can repeat it. If you want to create long-term, sustained success, you need to have confidence and certainty that you can repeat the same actions to produce the same result. An elite sports player, for example, gets paid a huge salary because they consistently perform at an outstanding level. They didn't just do it once or twice in practice; they do it all the time. 'Outstanding' is their base level and their meta programmes push them to aim higher. I often tell our team ahead of big events or challenges, 'You don't rise to the occasion, you sink to the level of your training.' We want to set the highest level of success as our minimum standard. We want to develop and implement the mindset that excellence is just part of who we are.

To achieve that mindset, we have to introduce repeatable processes. These actions need to be formulated as a series of activities that are consistently repeated, again and again and again. In an NLP context, we would refer to this as modelling. Modelling is where we find a real-life example of the success we want to achieve and then reverse-engineer their strategies. This allows us to quickly learn the things that matter and those that don't.

When I started WILD Success in 2013, although I was $40,000 in debt, I went on to make $100,000 in the first ninety days. How? I modelled the strategies of running a successful business, based on my mentor,

Chris Howard. I followed the exact steps that he outlined for me to take and I implemented the exact behaviours he said would be required. If you follow the same path, you'll arrive at the same destination.

As the earlier gambling example highlights, while it's important to do the hard work of creating new habits, it is equally crucial to dissolve the negative habits that we have allowed to creep into our lives. If you don't tip the scale in favour of your positive habits, you're never going to succeed or achieve the life of your dreams. What does neuroscience tell us about how to do that? There are two great books that I recommend you check out as resources on this complex topic. The first is *Atomic Habits* by James Clear and the second is *The Power of Habit,* by Charles Duhigg, the Pulitzer Prize-winning reporter and author. In the latter, Duhigg outlines that to create a new 'habit' or conditioned response, we need to take consistent, intentional action for sixty-six days.[45] After this amount of time, our brain's neurochemistry becomes hard-wired for the new behaviour and it's established as our new normal. There's nothing complicated about this, it's simply about doing the work. It's about showing up for the next nine to ten weeks and being intentional about who you want to be and how you want to interact with the world. Going through some of the big ideas from *The Power of Habit* can help you understand your habits and get started with the process of changing them. The crux of Duhigg's

---

45 Duhigg, C, *The Power of Habit: Why we do what we do and how to change* (Random House, 2014)

work suggests that there are three elements to every habit, positive or negative: the cue, the routine and the reward.

The cue is the spark, or the motivating factor. We don't always do things because we want to; often we're triggered by an underlying emotion or a belief system. For example, when Duhigg studied Alcoholics Anonymous, he found that people drink to excess not because they want to drink but because of an emotional trigger. Whether that trigger is loss, loneliness, isolation, boredom or even wanting to celebrate, every time they get that emotional cue, they repeat the same routine of reaching for the bottle. The only way to break the addiction is to identify the cue and then replace the routine and the reward that follows with something positive. If you ignore the emotional triggers that fuel your behaviour, the behavioural change that you need will evade you. This is why I keep repeating myself about the importance of creating awareness.

The second element, the routine, is often referred to as 'the behaviour'. Often, when people want to change a behaviour, they save it for a New Year's resolution. The resolution is often to exercise more, stick to a diet or save money. The reason these resolutions tend to fail is because they are all dependent upon routines that need to be cultivated over time. They're not something that you do casually or occasionally – quite the opposite, these are activities that you must do consistently and repeatedly to make them routine.

The final part of the process is the reward, which is the pay-off for completing the routine. The reward can be positive or negative. It's a process that happens inside our brain to reinforce that we've successfully completed a habit or routine. We need to be aware of both the positive and negative rewards that are present in our lives. If you have a routine of overeating, the reward could be a feeling of comfort, of feeling satiated or relaxed at the end of the day. I know plenty of people who have smoked marijuana, even though they know it's not serving them at their highest level, because they get the reward of feeling relaxed, calm or blissed out for a while. The reward is the high that we're chasing in our lives.

To change negative routines so that you are no longer a victim of self-defeating behaviour, Duhigg suggests that we implement a technique he refers to as 'the detour'. It's very simple. Imagine you drive to work the same way every day, but one day there are roadworks and you have to take a detour. It's a bit frustrating and might add a little time to your journey, but you follow the signposts and wait for the roadworks to end so that you can return to your old route. As it turns out, you're not given a choice because the road you used to take no longer exists. After some time, whether it's days, weeks or months, you find yourself driving along the new route automatically, as if you'd never taken another route before. How did that happen? Your brain, due to a process called 'automaticity', has become hard-wired so that it becomes more difficult to not follow your routine than to follow it.

WILD EXERCISE: Take a detour

Think for a moment: what are some of the autopilot routines or behaviours you would like to take conscious control over? Next, think about some detours that you can put in place to initiate a shift.

List five negative behaviours	Detours could you take
Eg working late and eating takeaway	Eg ordering food before the store closes or having a protein shake
1.	1.
2.	2.
3.	3.
4.	4.
5.	5.

A common positive detour that people use to replace a negative habit is exercise. Not only does it give a tremendous high (exercise releases endorphins), it's also something positive that can quickly become ritualistic. There are also health and emotional benefits, which lead to general wellbeing improvements.

A 2013 study from University College London showed that it typically takes sixty-six days to build the automaticity I referred to above.[46] In our NLP pro-

---

46 UCL Staff, 'How long does it take to form a habit?', (UCL News, 2009), www.ucl.ac.uk/news/2009/aug/how-long-does-it-take-form-habit, accessed 17 May 2022

grammes and training sessions, we teach a variety of strategies that help with the challenge of changing your habits. For example, we have a technique called a 'momentum pattern' that allows you to complete that sixty-six-day process effectively in about fifteen minutes. Using a momentum pattern is about training your nervous system to associate a new pattern with any given experience, as opposed to the old one, using advanced visualisation tools and future pacing. There are also ways to dissolve negative behaviours and emotions using a similar principle. One example of that is called a strategy scrambler. It's exciting, and we have used these tools to help people dealing with a range of problems, from anxiety to post-traumatic stress disorder. To learn more about these NLP tools, visit www.wildsuccess.global/book.

Changing any problematic habit in your life requires two things: self-awareness and a new behaviour to replace the old one. The self-awareness allows you to recognise the behaviours you currently exhibit and determine whether they fall on the green or red line. More importantly, that awareness will help you identify and implement new behaviours that will take you closer to your goals and dreams. The key to success is to change what you do on a daily basis and continually implement that change day after day after day. It's also important to recognise that if you want to leap from successful to extraordinary, the behaviours, routines and rituals that got you to your current level of success are not going to be the same ones that will get you to your next level of success.

If you adjust your behaviour today, nothing's going to change. Going to the gym today won't change a thing. But if you go to the gym again tomorrow, the impact will be greater. If you commit to going to the gym consistently for the next twelve months, you're going to have a completely different body. On a day-to-day basis, your behaviours, routines and rituals might seem inconsequential but the compound effect of long-term commitment to your goals is huge. First, because you benefit – in this case mentally, physically and physiologically from your workout – and second, because each day that you repeat it, that new behaviour, routine or ritual is an investment in the person you want to become.

Interview: Karim El Barche

Karim El Barche is an international fitness model, award-winning entrepreneur and marketing executive. Karim has been featured in *Australian Iron Man* magazine and on the cover of *Men's Muscle & Health*. After incredible success at the 2013 World Fitness Model Championships, Karim scaled and grew his Melbourne-based fitness business Discovery Health and Fitness to new heights. This led to more than a decade of peak performance coaching and thousands of successful transformations.

Karim is currently pursuing a master's degree in marketing at the University of Melbourne. He has redefined the standard of excellence in all areas of my life, is one of my closest friends and a remarkable man. In the interview below, we talk about the physical proof of powerful behaviours.

Calvin: What does 'living a WILD life' mean to you?

Karim: To me, living a WILD life is about many things. First, it's about believing in possibility, in having big dreams and doing what you can to achieve them. Second, it's about having resilience, patience and understanding that goals and dreams take time. Third, it's being able to acknowledge that there will be sacrifices along the way. Living a WILD life is having the audacity to chase the life that you want.

On a day-to-day basis, it's about doing what you love to do – whatever that looks like. For me, those are simple things like training, eating, working, studying, learning and travelling. It's chipping away at the long-term goals and taking satisfaction from making progress.

Calvin: What is the primary habit, routine or ritual you follow that has the greatest impact on your life?

Karim: Without a doubt, my training. I have a daily ritual of hitting the gym and lifting weights. To many, that may sound over-simplified or silly but to me it's my most important ritual. I am an athlete and I always will be. This is the single most powerful driving force that has allowed me to overcome the challenges life can throw at you. Not only that, but I also just really enjoy it. I love the challenge and the constant pursuit.

The training also sets up other rituals around nutrition, sleep and rest.

Calvin: How has this habit helped you achieve your current level of success?

Karim: Training and sport are a part of who I am. It's a part of my identity and there is no scenario in which I wouldn't make it a part of my life. For as long as I have the physical capacity to train, I will. To give you an example, my grandfather is eighty-two and still rides his bike hundreds of kilometres per week up hills and mountains that would put us all to shame. I hope that this habit will always be a part of my life. It's programmed into my DNA and I just love it. It has helped me because it gives me something to look forward to.

Calvin: What is your recommendation for someone who is trying to implement powerful habits into their lives? How do they make that big shift toward being aware of their negative habits and actively implementing positive ones?

Karim: I think, from a habit perspective, it's not so much about trying to identify bad habits and then breaking them, it's more about optimising. Ask yourself, 'How can I be better at this? What do I need to learn, implement or set up to improve at this? Who can I learn from?' Beyond that, if you're genuinely stuck on something, I recommend meditation as a tool to help with awareness. Meditation gives you a chance to stop and take stock of what's going on, to see things from a new perspective. Like anything, it takes work and requires a committed effort.

Calvin: How did finding a mentor impact your journey?

Karim: Mentors have played an influential role in my life. I think the key is finding mentors who you share similar values with and creating relationships where you both bring something to the table. Mentors can offer guidance when you are unclear of how to move forward. Similarly, a good student can be rewarding for a mentor, as they get to see you progress and succeed. If you find the right relationship, it can be mutually rewarding.

Calvin: How do your health and wellness rituals contribute to your success in that field?

Karim: I am someone who thrives on routine; I like doing the same things over and over. In many ways, this has allowed me to be successful in health and fitness because I've built a foundation of daily habits that rarely change. Each day I'll wake up, often do a meditation, eat, have a coffee, work, train, eat, work, eat, go for a walk and go to bed. Other things will slot in but, for the most part, that's my routine – in that exact order. The rest of my life revolves around that routine, not the other way around. If you want to be more successful in health and fitness, find a way to make it fun and spend time with other people who are doing it well.

8
Obsessive Focus

Imagine you're casually swiping through Tinder. You spot a nicely dressed, attractive person. Of course, you swipe right. Much to your delight, it's a match. This happened to Norwegian woman Cecilie Fjellhøy, who believed her Prince Charming (who had just invited her to join him on his private jet) was the son of a diamond magnate. The next several weeks for her were a whirlwind of luxury, romance and all the love-filled promises she'd ever wanted to hear. Then things changed. She's now $200,000 in debt, Prince Charming isn't returning her calls and the last cheque he sent just bounced. Cecilie found herself living that nightmare just thirteen weeks after believing she had met the love of her life. She and two other victims shared their stories in the Netflix true-crime documentary, *The Tinder Swindler*.

The Tinder Swindler was the first documentary to climb to the top of Netflix's weekly viewing chart.[47] It follows the story of alleged con man Shimon Hayut, who assumes the name Simon Leviev, and exposes the secrets of his complex scheme. I think this documentary went viral for two reasons. First, is the popularity of Tinder itself. It's the world's most popular app, topping download charts for 2021 and currently hosting more than 75 million active users.[48] It's easy to see then how viewers would be captivated by a story they could picture themselves starring in and relieved that they'd managed to avoid it. Second, these viewers, passively watching this nightmare unfold, were eager to judge the victims for what they saw as obvious stupidity. 'Who jumps on a private jet with someone they just met on Tinder? How stupid.' Ultimately, though, this has nothing to do with the women who fell victim to Leviev and everything to do with confirmation bias.

The limitations of focus

Confirmation bias is a result of how our brain filters and processes information. It highlights information that goes along with our preferred narrative and deletes anything that goes against it. This is a powerful

---

47   White, P, '"The Tinder Swindler" becomes Netflix's most-watched documentary', (Deadline, 2022), https://deadline.com/2022/04/tinder-swindler-netflix-1235005966, accessed 17 May 2022

48   Iqbal, M, 'Tinder revenue and usage statistics (2022)', (Business of Apps, 2022), www.businessofapps.com/data/tinder-statistics, accessed 17 May 2022

tool; there's a lot of information around you, so your brain has become tremendously adept at narrowing your field of view so you only focus on, and indeed see, what (it thinks) matters. The inherent risk with this is that you could delete something significant without even thinking about it.

The way we form first impressions is an excellent example of this, which is explored in a study by Princeton psychologists Janine Willis and Alexander Todorov.[49] After performing a series of experiments, they determined that we form a first impression of a stranger after looking at their face for just one-tenth of a second.

Each of five experiments focused on a different personality trait: attractiveness, likeability, competence, trustworthiness and aggressiveness. Photographs of unfamiliar faces were shown to participants for varying times (some for one-tenth of a second, some for half a second and some for a full second) and they then had to judge each face against each trait – eg 'Is this person attractive/likeable/competent/trustworthy/aggressive?'. Participants were also asked to rate their own confidence in the judgement they had made. This set of results was compared with the results of a preliminary study where the participants had been given no time constraints to answer.

The result of the comparison showed that an increase in time did not increase accuracy – judgements

---

49 Willis, J and Todorov, A, 'First impressions: Making up your mind after a 100-ms exposure to a face', *Psychological Science*, 17/7 (2006), 592–598, https://doi.org/10.1111/j.1467-9280.2006.01750.x

were highly correlated between both sets of results, but there was an increase in the confidence felt by the participants of their own judgements.

In simple terms, people had already made up their minds in the one-tenth of a second and then used the rest of the time to reinforce that decision – in other words, confirmation bias. Consider that in the example of *The Tinder Swindler*, Leviev is strategic in first meeting his dates (ie targets) in five-star hotels, driving them around in limousines and even taking them on a private jet for an impromptu second date. By building a carefully constructed image of wealth and opulence, coupled with a fake online profile, he conditions his victims into thinking he's the real deal. Little do they know that this façade is funded by the previous innocent victim he'd used the same tricks on.

Once a first impression has been formed, it's hard to destroy because our brain then magnifies everything that fits our narrative and deletes anything that goes against the grain. Science tells us that the human brain can process 11 million bits of information per second,[50] but our conscious minds can only handle around 40 to 120 bits of information per second.[51] While you're reading or listening to this book, you're dealing with all manner of distractions. There are so

---

50 Miller, GA, 'The magical number seven, plus or minus two: Some limits on our capacity for processing information, *Psychological Review*, 63/2 (1956), 81–97. https://doi.org/10.1037/h0043158
51 'How much RAM does the human brain have?', (Neurotray, 2022), https://neurotray.com/how-much-ram-does-the-human-brain-have, accessed 20 April 2023

many stimuli being received by your brain it has to do one of three things: delete, distort or generalise the information. While you're looking at or listening to my words, you're probably not aware of the beating heart in your chest, the feeling of your body sitting on the chair or your feet snuggled into your shoes. But now you are – because I've put those thoughts into your mind, you're directing your focus to those areas of your body. To take the example further, even though you are now thinking about your body against the chair, you're not specifically thinking, 'My body is resting against the black chair with armrests.' You're not thinking of your feet in the shoes that are white with an icon on the side and tied-up laces because your brain simply generalises these items into the category of 'chair' and 'shoe', to keep life simple. Your brain recognises the general pattern and skims over the details. The downside to this is that we can lose the ability to notice and experience the nuances of new things.

Of the 11 million bits of information coming at your nervous system at any given time, studies have shown that 83% of it is received by the visual receptors, your eyes. The brain filters the information and you're left with 40 to 120 bits of data that you can consciously process at one time. We cluster that into five to nine areas of focus – for example, your partner, kids, work, health and finances. This is why people who are asked to list brands of cars, flavours of soda, friends and family members can easily give five to nine responses without having to think too hard about it, but coming up with a list beyond that requires more thought. For this reason, Apple's Steve Jobs supposedly never had more than seven direct reports. He understood that we can't effectively handle more than seven areas of focus at one time. I do need to point out, however, that this number dates from 1952. A more recent study suggests that we are now limited to a maximum of four things that we can focus on at any given time.[52]

While we may not be able to eliminate every bias or multitask as much as we'd like, there are steps we can take to harness and maximise the power we have over our focus.

Cultivating obsessive focus

As we've seen, you're only ever taking in a fraction of the information coming at you, an amount so small that a large majority of the world around you is being blocked out. You're simply not aware of it. You don't see the world as it is – you see the world as you already are. If you want to change the results you're getting in your life, you need to change the way you see the world by actively shifting your attention to what you want to focus on.

---

52 Moskowitz, C, 'Mind's limit found: 4 things at once', (LiveScience, 2008), www.livescience.com/2493-mind-limit-4.html, accessed 17 May 2022

WILD EXERCISE: Controlling your focus

Changing how you see the world is easier said than done. In this exercise, I provide three simple steps to help you take conscious control of your focus.

Step One: Bring awareness to your current areas of focus.

It can be hard to identify your focus areas, so I suggest asking a close friend for their input. Ask them what they think you're focused on based on what you talk about, complain about and what kinds of things seem to grab your attention. Ask them what topics repeatedly come up with you and which of those seem to bring you joy or push your buttons. Don't take the answers to heart; they reflect who you used to be, not who you are becoming. Using their insights as a benchmark, consider what subjects, people or issues have taken up most of your focus, time, energy and attention over the past three to six months and write them down.

Step Two: Decide with intention what you want to focus on.

Many people major in minor subjects in life. They spread their attention thin to cover a lot of things that don't matter, as opposed to concentrating their attention on the few things that do. In his landmark book *Think and Grow Rich*,[53] Napoleon Hill identified that the successful people he interviewed all had one thing in common, a trait he referred to as 'a single-mindedness of purpose'. He found that successful people focused on one thing to the elimination of everything else.

---

53 Hill, N, *Think and Grow Rich* (Vermillion, 2004)

Consider what you want your life to be like over the next five to ten years. Ask yourself, 'What four things do I need to focus on above everything else?' Identify which focus areas are the most likely to create that success and write them down.

Step Three: Condition yourself to return to those focus areas over the next sixty to ninety days. Make them visible, write lists, create mantras, whatever works for you to keep those four things top of mind. Does this sound easier said than done? That's because it is. Keep reading...

Imagine if, like a radio station, you could tune your brain into the frequency of these four things and drown out the noise of everything else. Imagine how much more focused and productive you would be, how many more ideas you would have and how minimal the distractions and useless thoughts that crowd your thinking would be. If only there were a part of your brain built to do just this. Thankfully, there is. It's called the Reticular Activating System (RAS). This part of the brain behaves much like the captain of a ship. It steers your focus toward the most important information for you based on the parameters of your current focus and then shines a big searchlight on it so you can't miss it. If you've ever had the experience of shopping around for a new car then seeing your preferred model everywhere, you'll know what I'm talking about. If you've ever bought a new pair of shoes, handbag or outfit only to notice someone wearing the same thing, you'll know what I'm talking about. If you've ever had a conversation about someone and then bumped into them later that day or week, you'll know what I'm talking about. This is your RAS in action. It's the spotlight in your mind that allows you to pick up on the things that you are unconsciously focused on. The good news is, you can train this sense to become even sharper.

Refer to the list above of your four new focus areas. I'd love to say that your RAS will now take over and you never have to think about anything else for the rest of your life – if only it were that simple. Just because you've selected and identified what you want to focus on, doesn't mean change is immediate. Think of the process working like a search engine. The Google search engine has a front part (the search box) and a behind-the-scenes part (the algorithm). You don't see the algorithm working but it's the most powerful component of the Google brand. When you type keywords into Google, you're stating your intention or your preference – you're telling Google what you want it to focus on, much like you do with your RAS. When you put love, wealth, prosperity, abundance, health or vitality into the RAS search engine, you're going to immediately search the world around you for those things. Just because you're searching for those things, doesn't mean you're going to get results right away – your current algorithm needs new data.

If you went online and searched the term 'health', your results would be different from anyone else's. This is because Google tailors the results to what is most relevant based on your previous searches and browsing history. You're already getting tailored results – this is good if they are relevant, quality results but bad if you want new information right now. The same process happens in your brain. Your brain is an incredible pattern-recognising machine. When you state new intentions like wealth, prosperity or abundance, don't be surprised when you see more examples of lack or people struggling in the world. You are seeing more examples of your own experiences of scarcity and frustration with regard to money because your current algorithm, due to your previous search patterns and histories, has been one of lack and scarcity.

To ingrain a new paradigm, we need to work at both the conscious and subconscious levels of your current conditioning. In our seminars and events, we use a variety of tools to help people break though their subconscious blocks and barriers. This is akin to clearing your browser history and starting afresh. An immediate, short-term hack that works to reprogram your subconscious is saving your goals as a screen-saver on your desktop and smartphone. The average person picks up their phone nearly 100 times a day. Those 100 pick-ups can take on a functional purpose by ensuring top-of-mind awareness of your goals. That is just one approach – use the tools that will work best for you. If you need a sticky note rainbow, make it; if you need to add them as mantras to your daily meditation, speak them out loud; if you need to tattoo them on your leg like Guy Pearce in *Memento*, go for it.

The following exercise is a great way of bringing conscious awareness to what you, and those around you, focus on.

WILD EXERCISE: Expanding your lens

Consider the week you've just had and choose an experience that you can reflect on in both a positive and negative way. Now frame that experience within these opposing viewpoints: how would your most positive friend narrate this experience and how would your most negative friend narrate this experience? Then, reach out to those friends, share the experience and ask for their input. Try to get them to expand on the areas they found positive or negative. Note the key points that they focus on. These are the different lenses through which you can view your experience; you can use these in a deliberate way to create an entirely different experience.

Interview: Andrew Pearce

Andrew is a professional coach and mentor who has been studying personal growth, consciousness, spirituality, shadow work and more since 2014. Andrew supports deep healing and transformation in those who desire a life of freedom, balance, travel, purpose and adventure.

With personal experiences of stress, anxiety, burnout and dysfunctional busy-ness, Andrew has been able to uncover the core insights and healing necessary to guide change in his clients so that they can create for themselves and experience a life of purpose. In the below interview, I talk to him about bringing your resistance into focus.

Calvin: What does 'living a WILD life' mean to you?

Andrew: It means living life on my own terms; it means having the ability to do what I want to do, when I want to do it. It is doing meaningful work and having meaningful relationships. It is the ability to work from anywhere and, more than that, it is doing the work that you love and having that work support the lifestyle that you want.

Living life on my own terms means feeling emotionally fulfilled and satisfied with what I do, who I am and the people I have in my life. It means having hobbies, interests and activities outside of work that I do purely for enjoyment, which gives me opportunities for growth and contribution.

Calvin: How have focus and calming the mind helped you to overcome the challenges you've faced personally and professionally?

Andrew: It's allowed me to become aware of the unconscious limiting beliefs that have led me down the paths of self-sabotage, avoidance strategies and procrastination. Recognising these limiting beliefs and then processing and releasing them has allowed me to upgrade my belief system and access more of my innate potential. This kind of internal work results in more aligned action, which then attracts more opportunities and experiences into my life that support my forward momentum toward the achievement of my goals.

Calvin: What are the biggest mistakes you see clients make when it comes to their ability to focus and manage their internal dialogue?

Andrew: The biggest mistake I see clients make is that they are afraid of negativity. They're afraid of fear, they're afraid of pain, they're afraid of insecurity and they're afraid of self-doubt because they misunderstand the purpose of these emotions. This leads them to fight against and resist them. People try to force their positivity. They try to make themselves feel grateful when they aren't; they try to push away self-doubt and focus on what they think they 'should' focus on. This only slows them down. What we resist persists and the energies that we fight, we feed.

Calvin: What tools would you recommend to someone who wants to take back control of their focus and mindset?

Andrew: The most important tool I would recommend is meditation and, with that, the understanding that there's no such thing as a good or bad meditation. Meditation is simply the nonjudgemental observation of your experience. It's allowing yourself space to feel how you're feeling; to stop fighting how you're feeling. Meditation is a surrender to the feelings, emotions and doubts that are in your body. It's removing the resistance, waving the white flag of surrender and stopping the fight.

Meditation is an incredible place to start and then I would also recommend doing some somatic work. Somatic work is getting into our body – with NLP you can do work to help change a negative into a positive, but that doesn't always allow you to fully process the negative energy and emotion behind that limiting belief. Doing somatic work to release the negative energy and emotion is the most effective way to expel those residuals from your body.

Calvin: How has mentorship helped you in your journey to challenge your patterns and embrace new ways of thinking?

Andrew: Mentorship or coaching is the fast-track from A to B. A mentor is someone who's been there, done that before; someone who can see where your blocks are, who can provide the insights that will open your thinking, your awareness and your consciousness, and take you to the next level. A mentor is someone who has already figured it out, who has walked the path you are currently on and who has the answers that you are seeking. Access to that level of support has helped me get where I want to go faster.

It's helped me by continually pointing me in the right direction, both for the internal work that I need to do to grow and evolve and for the external actions and strategies that I need to implement to get the results I want.

9
Proven Strategy

We have now arrived at a crucial crossroads on our WILD journey. We have covered a lot of ground, discovered a great selection of tools and now we're about to confront the most dangerous beast in the wild: the unknown. Let me ask you this: do you consider yourself a survivor? Could you land on a deserted island, survey the landscape and find the materials for basic survival, such as water, the components of fire, shelter and food? Or, in that situation, do you think you might find yourself in a state of panic, regretting not paying closer attention to all those episodes of *Survivor* or *Alone* that you watched?

Let's assume you overcome this panic, your survival instincts kick in and you manage to make a few rushed, and probably lucky, decisions that keep you safe and alive for your first night stranded and alone.

Maybe you end up drinking water that isn't totally safe so you get sick, or you find mushrooms and berries but can't be sure they're safe to eat so you end up going to sleep hungry. You do find some large, wide leaves and decide to lay them out as a mat to sleep on instead of lying down in the sand. How much better can you expect to do if you have zero survivalist knowledge?

An experience like that might make you think to yourself, 'Hmm, maybe I should learn some survival skills in case I ever find myself in a position like that again.' So you binge a few series of *Man vs Wild*, *Survivorman* and *Man, Woman, Wild* because on these shows Bear Grylls, Les Stroud and Mykel Hawke and his wife Ruth England prove that they know how to handle themselves and the terrain around them. They each have backgrounds that have forged them into self-sufficient, tough, problem-solving, survival experts. That is the kind of knowledge I would want to acquire to better equip myself for the next time I found myself stranded and alone.

Each of these experts provides 'how tos' for getting out of desperate situations. Each 'how to' provides information about the tools you need and proven methods for implementing those tools. They have collectively encountered or re-enacted all possible survival situations you may ever be unlucky enough to find yourself in. The combination of knowledge and experience they have gives these experts excellent credibility as mentors or guides for exploring the wild. Having access to this kind of knowledge, you would be unlikely to think, 'Okay, I've watched one episode of *Man vs Wild*, I'll just throw a few things into a go bag, a hammer, maybe a can of Coke, a towel and my mobile phone, and I'll be set for survival.' Reading that, it sounds ridiculous, so why do so many of us seem to make crucial decisions about our lives in exactly that way? When you set a goal, why are you (to follow the metaphor) haphazardly throwing useless supplies in your bag, pulling out whatever you've got on hand and just having a crack? Why would you not seek out a mentor or, in this case, a survivalist who you could watch and learn from to understand their methods, tools and ideas? This would allow you to shortcut past the trial-and-error process and make sure you stand a chance of surviving on your own. An even better option is to go with your guide out into the wild and get first-hand experience by learning what they do and how they do it.

Why do you need a proven strategy?

Think of your goals as quests. Who is your guide and what essentials do you need to pack before you embark? This is particularly important when you're attempting something you've never done before. Things like grocery shopping or driving home from work aren't quests because you do them all the time. On the other hand, if you're travelling to another country where they speak a foreign language, it makes sense to hire a tour guide. It makes no sense to me that people have health and fitness goals but don't go to a trainer for aligned strategies around nutrition and exercise. In the same way, I can't understand why someone who wants to achieve financial success assumes they're just going to figure it out on their own without the help of a financial expert. The reality is, if you want to turn decades into days, if you want to fast-track your life and achieve great things, you need to start spending time with people who have achieved similarly great things. Those successful people will have also spent time with other successful people and, as a result, they can share valuable wisdom about how to achieve your own version of success. Proximity equals power.

As you follow in the footsteps of those who have already achieved success, you will learn the survival skills, tools and strategies required to understand the environment around you. When you're thinking about who to align with, remember this simple rule: never take advice from somebody you wouldn't want to trade places with. If you're following somebody and they're not living the best version of the life you want to live, find a new guide. This mentality is relevant in every area of your life, but none so much as your peer group – because peer pressure is real. We need to choose our peers wisely because, as American entrepreneur Jim Rohn says, you are the average of the top five people you hang out with.[54]

54 Groth, A, 'You're the average of the five people you spend the most time with', (*Business Insider*, 2012), www.businessinsider.com/ jim-rohn-youre-the-average-of-the-five-people-you-spend-the-most-time-with-2012-7, accessed 21 June 2021

In 2017, I was returning from a tour in Brisbane. As I was refuelling the rental car at the airport, I noticed three guys in a truck wearing the high-visibility gear required at a mine site. Now, it's 9am and two of the three guys have a meat pie, a sausage roll and an energy drink. Imagine you're the guy in the back of the vehicle and you've decided to go on a health kick – you have a sparkling water and a salad. Even if his friends are supportive, the guy in the back is spending the drive smelling the pie and craving his usual energy drink. Chances are that his next choice won't be aligned with his goals. It's also more likely that the friends are not going to be supportive and he will ultimately end up giving up the health kick. The people in our lives can either empower or disempower us, so it's important that we choose them wisely.

I've been able to grow successful companies that make millions of dollars, develop my business to impact more lives, fall in love and remain in a beautiful, committed relationship, have high levels of physical energy and vitality (despite interrupted sleep with a newborn at home) and achieve the body of my dreams. I don't get to live life on my own terms because I was born with these things; I am able to achieve success because I found mentors and guides who provided me with the skills and the methodology to excel in each of these areas. This is the power of mentorship. Without mentorship, you will find yourself falling into the same traps as everyone else. It is one thing to have the courage to step into the wild, it's another thing to make sure you don't get lost.

The wild can be a dangerous place if you don't have the support of a strong tribe.

Identifying your strategy

Before we can design your dream strategy, we need to look at your current strategy to find out what is working for or against you. People say to me all the time, 'Calvin, I don't know where I'm going in life.' I say to them, 'Let's find out where you're going to end up.' I do this by looking at their financial statements for the past ninety days alongside their personal calendar, which tells me how they spent their time and what they achieved each day, week and month. I also ask about what they've put into their body, how they felt emotionally and what they were thinking about each day. With these factors combined, we can get an incredible snapshot of their current strategy. Because we are creatures of habit and most of our neurological pathways are pre-set by the time we reach thirty, I can also tell them that their future is a well-rehearsed past.

If you've been unable to save money in the past ninety days, there's a good chance you're not going to be able to do it in the next ninety days, or any period after that. If you haven't been able to get yourself to the gym in the past ninety days, there's a good chance you're not going to do it moving forward. If you haven't been able to eat the right foods, there's a good chance that's not going to change – unless something else changes. This might sound harsh, but remember; if nothing changes, nothing changes!

Believe me, I've been through this. I remember feeling frustrated that I wasn't making enough progress in my life. I was just getting started in my business and my goal was to make a million dollars in my first year (yes, it was a huge goal – remember: aim for what you want). I was failing miserably. One day, I was venting and complaining to my dad about all the things that were going wrong and I remember him saying to me, 'Son, you're just not good enough. You're not good enough to run a million-dollar business.' At the time, those words felt like a slap in the face. I felt like saying, 'How dare you say that to me? I'm trying to make something happen here.' Seeing the look on my face, he continued, 'Hold on. Don't react. Just understand what I've said. It's obvious to me you don't yet have the skills, the tools or the talent to run a million-dollar business because you don't yet have one. Instead of trying to build a million-dollar business, why don't you work on becoming a man who *can* run a million-dollar business? Then, surely, you will have one. I'm not saying you're not good enough. I'm saying you're not good enough *yet*. You need to work on your skills and emotions to become good enough.'

I realised something in that moment: I needed to find a mentor. I needed to seek out someone who had forged a path from starting a business to running a million-dollar company. I needed to find somebody who could teach me strategies to replace my frustration with calm and my overwhelm with ease and grace.

Someone who could help me understand the journey ahead so I didn't feel frustrated. With that kind of instruction, I'd have a plan of action, a proven strategy to take me from where I was to where I wanted to be. In the coming pages, I'm going to share with you the single most important piece of advice I learned from the mentor I sought out after that epiphany, advice that allowed me to make a million dollars within ten months. If you pay attention to what I'm about to share, it can help you do the same.

A mentor is the shortcut to mastery

This mentor shared with me two key ideas: first, that what got you here won't get you there; and second, that the fastest way to get from where you are to where you want to be is to find someone who has already done it and do what they did. I mentioned earlier that to understand how to get where you want to go, we have to first understand your current strategy. Tony Robbins breaks down three types of strategists.[55] For anyone who isn't familiar with this, I'll summarise. We have the dabblers, the stress-achievers and the masters. When you're reading through the following explanation, consider which type resonates with you the most. Which pattern of behaviour do you think you demonstrate?

---

55 Robbins, T, 'The difference between a master, a stressor, and a dabbler is what they do when they get to a plateau', (Facebook Watch, 2014), www.facebook.com/watch/?v=10152682303459060&ref=sharing, accessed 17 May 2022

Let's start with the dabbler. A dabbler has a short attention span and is always distracted by the latest shiny thing in their life. They're someone who is constantly procrastinating and hesitating. They are always starting something new – a new project, a new relationship, a new financial plan, a new diet or a new money-making scheme and, within days or weeks, their initial bright spark fizzles out. Their motivation disappears when they get to the hard work part and they quit, only to start something new. For example, they could be constantly 'yo-yo dieting' because they don't develop good, solid lifestyle habits. They might be forever jumping from job to job because, after a while, the job gets boring or they're up for a performance review and decide to bail before they face feedback or criticism. They are always in need of new and fresh stimulation. Their pattern looks like the figure below.

Result

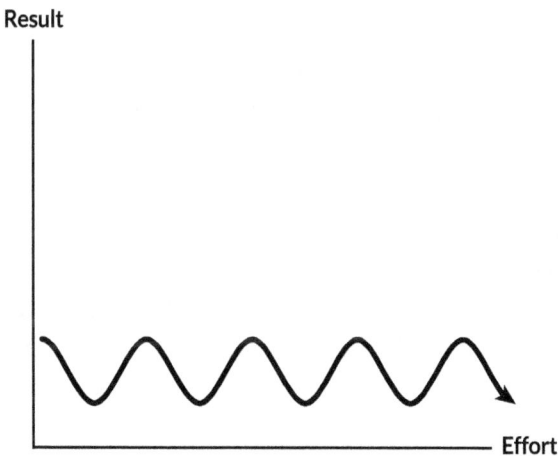

Effort

Consider this trait in someone who's addicted to sugar. In the beginning, when they're tasting something new and sweet, they will get a rush of excitement from the burst of flavour. Long term, they risk becoming overweight or developing diabetes because they sacrifice making healthy choices for the rush of finding new and more exciting sweet treats. For dabblers, the short-term game is the only one they know how to play. They're constantly trying to find the instant fix, the get-rich-quick scheme or the miracle diet that will get them to the finish line fastest. But they do this without considering the benefits of developing the lifestyle skills, tools, habits and resources that create lasting results. The result is short-term excitement and long-term misery. To truly create the life of your dreams, you must grow and develop into a person worthy of living that life. If you keep quitting on yourself, you'll never get there.

Next are the stress-achievers who, as their name suggests, waste their productive energy being stressed and anxious. They live in the future, always looking for what's next and are rarely anchored in the present moment. They are never satisfied, always impatient and running full steam ahead while trying to do everything at once. They're overwhelmed and overworked but they wear those labels like a badge of honour. These are the people who brag about hustling all the time and never stopping, not even for sleep. A stress-achiever is fuelled by the idea of not just achieving but achieving with less than everybody else – less sleep, less money, less time and less support. They wear their struggle proudly because stress-achievers want to succeed and achieve, which would be excellent if it wasn't for the fact that they do it in such an unhealthy way, as illustrated in the figure below.

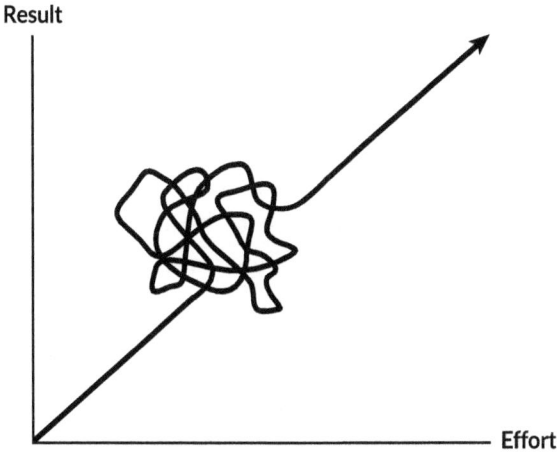

They use pressure, stress and the fear of not being good enough to motivate them to reach the next level. When you speak to a stress-achiever, you won't hear them talk about having depression or anxiety. They talk about stress and pressure, which really is the same thing just described differently. When they're not making progress, when they feel as though they're plateauing or flatlining, they get incredibly frustrated. The solution for most stress-achievers when they're in that place is to do more work. They tend to think, 'If I'm working ten hours a day, five days a week and not achieving my goals, then I'm going to have to up it to twelve, fourteen, sixteen or eighteen hours a day, seven days a week to achieve what I want.' They see it as an effort-based problem. Stress-achievers don't consider that they might have the wrong tools or that they are using the wrong methodology. They just think they aren't trying hard enough.

When stress-achievers look around them, they either see people succeeding or people quitting. They look at the people dabbling and can attribute their lack of success to them being 'quitters' with a poor work ethic. When they look to the people succeeding, they assume they have to keep the pressure on and keep pushing through the pain, so they try even harder until... hello burnout.

A stress-achiever leaves behind a trail of collateral damage. There will be destruction: of their body (perhaps they suffer from chronic fatigue or breakdowns), of their finances (they might run up debt while chasing financial freedom), of their relationships (where they cut people off to rid themselves of distraction, or don't make time for them), or of their soul and spirit (because they've become so accustomed to working that they've forgotten about living).

Thankfully, there's another way – the Wild way: mastery. Understanding mastery requires that you accept the idea that our lives, like the seasons in nature, feature times of growth and times of retreat, times of expression and times of withdrawal. There are going to be times in your life, personally and professionally, when you grow and when you stagnate.

These are simply the seasons of life. You don't do the same thing or expect the same results in summer that you do in winter.

What's different about masters is that they understand what they want to accomplish and how to achieve it. They start with the enthusiasm of a dabbler and they persevere like a stress-achiever, but the energy they put into their journey is different. What they understand is that a true master is always a beginner. Each new goal is a new, different, winding path into the wild. Every great black belt has a white-belt mentality. They understand that there's always someone higher up the ladder of success than them. They're always trying to learn from whoever is above them. The process of mastery is a cycle – grow, stabilise and learn, grow, stabilise and learn – as illustrated in the figure below.

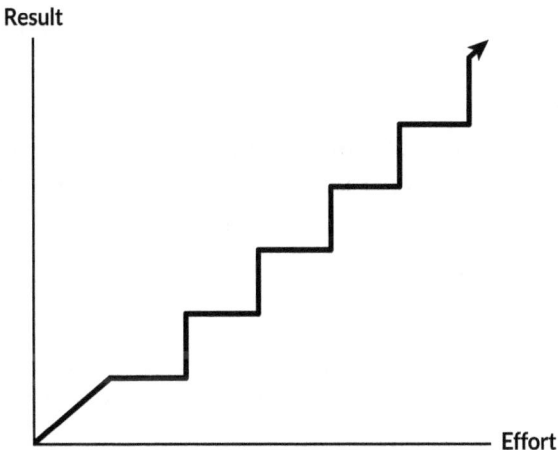

Arnold Schwarzenegger has done this well. He found mentors in bodybuilding and became Mr Olympia. He then found mentors in the movie industry and has been the highest-paid actor in the entertainment industry.[56] He found mentors in politics and held the seat of Governor of California for two terms.[57] When you master this process, you will have arrived at WILD Success. A strategy of mastery removes so much of the frustration, the challenge, the fear, the doubt and the worry from your life because you allow yourself to accept that there is already a path to success. All you have to do is follow the path and understand the timeline. Then, you'll find yourself in a position where you not only survive but you thrive.

Up to now, have you been living like a dabbler or a stressor, or have you been pursuing the path of mastery? The fact you're reading this book tells me you have the capacity and propensity to become masterful at whatever you do, to become a black belt and remain a white belt in your mind, to become the master who is always learning.

Because you're still reading this book, you're in a great position to get to the next level. Next, you need to find someone on the next rung of the ladder you're climbing and ask them how they got there. That's

---

56 Jones, B, 'Arnold Schwarzenegger net worth: Was Arnold Schwarzenegger the highest paid actor?', (Keeper Facts, 2022), https://keeperfacts.com/arnold-schwarzenegger-net-worth, accessed 21 May 2022

57 Waxman, S, 'From Pumping Iron to Pushing Political Ideas', (The Washington Post, 2003), www.washingtonpost.com/archive/politics/2003/09/28/from-pumping-iron-to-pushing-political-ideas/a82d38e7-a92d-47dd-b505-6fc8aa5cda19, accessed 30 May 2023

how you turn decades into days. Commit this mantra to memory: how you do anything is how you do everything. If you do this in your emotional life, you will do it in your financial life. If you do this with your money, you will do it in your relationships. If you do this in your relationships, you will do it with your body. All these interconnected efforts will determine your success or failure.

Interview: Elsa Morgan

Elsa was born into poverty, with two dining chairs acting as her bassinette. When she was eighteen months old, her parents decided to migrate to Australia in search of greater opportunities, but their finances did not improve. Without a pattern of success to follow, she struggled with managing money throughout her teens and early adulthood. She knew she wasn't passionate about her studies and dropped out of university. By the age of thirty, she had a string of failed relationships behind her and was heavily in debt. She lost all her savings during the global financial crisis and had to file for bankruptcy.

At forty, realising she had to rebuild her life, Elsa began her personal development journey. Along with finding love, getting married and bringing a son into the world, she discovered a fresh motivation and purpose in life. Putting this feeling of renewal out to the universe, she discovered the online business world through a network marketing contact and started learning how it all worked. Around the same time, a friend introduced her to WILD Success and our programmes. Starting from nothing, with no knowledge or money, Elsa told us she wanted to be the 'next seven-figure coach'. From that moment, she never looked back, taking every step on the way with a go-getter attitude.

Elsa was hungry for success and, although she had limiting beliefs at times, she didn't allow herself to give up. She is now running a successful business and looking to hire people to support its rapid growth. In four short months, Elsa has earned six figures and counting. Elsa's story demonstrates that anything is possible. In the interview below, I talk to her about how the right mindset and a proven strategy took her straight to success.

Calvin: What does 'living a WILD life' mean to you?

Elsa: As you say, a WILD life is living life on your own terms. That deeply resonates with me because it means I get to dictate how I live my life. I get to decide how I want to contribute to the world. Up until the point that I got started with WILD Success, I didn't believe I could do that because my history painted a very different picture of what was available to me.

Calvin: Can you pinpoint when you discovered that the strategy you had been following just wasn't working?

Elsa: I knew it wasn't working because I had no clue what I was going to do. I was working as a paid coach for a coaching company, earning less than $30 an hour and had a peak of eighty-one clients on my books at one time. I would just over-deliver and over-deliver and over-deliver and there were days that were fully booked with back-to-back, one-on-one sessions. The income wasn't the main issue; it was the burnout and imbalance I was beginning to experience that made me realise I had so much more to give. I knew that there had to be a better way but I had no idea how to get started. All I knew was what I knew as a paid coach – I didn't know what I didn't know, until I found WILD Success.

Calvin: How did you identify what wasn't working in order to change your path? And what would you recommend to someone who is trying to change their own direction?

Elsa: I'd been with the coaching company for about two years and I had toyed with the idea of starting my own. I identified a gap in the market for helping women over forty build businesses in my profession of coaching, network marketing and direct sales. I found that, for a lot of women over forty, the standard strategies weren't aligned with what that demographic wanted. It seemed that I could get results out of the over-forty clients because I was able to create a particularly good dynamic with them. I knew just by listening to my clients that the company's method wasn't working. My clients were doing well, but the other coaches and their clients weren't getting the same quality of results as rapidly, which told me that I was onto something. I just thought to myself, 'This isn't working.' When I find myself in that position, I know I need to go back to basics. I had to ask myself, 'Who are you really speaking to? Why are you doing this? And what's the outcome you want to achieve?' That is the thought process I would recommend to anyone feeling a similar helplessness. The necessary action is to go back to basics and those three key areas: Who are you speaking to? Why are you doing this? And what's the ultimate result?

From there, I had to push through, shift my mindset and shift the inner chatter that was listing all the reasons why I couldn't succeed. I kept pushing through until I started breaking new ground every single week. Naturally, I was hitting limiting beliefs but, at the same time, I felt like this was my one chance to do this properly.

Calvin: How did finding a mentor impact your journey?

Elsa: Finding a mentor absolutely made my journey. I'm an implementer so, if I'm given a strategy, if you tell me what I need to do, I'm going to go and do it. That's what I really enjoyed most about learning from you. It was literally a process of me listening to you tell me what to do and then I would just go and implement. Learning from a company like WILD Success was the most obvious thing for me. I was able to tap into the wisdom of someone who knew exactly how to move me from where I was to where I wanted to go.

One time, I had a mini-meltdown – I was in over-whelm and experiencing imposter syndrome – and I broke down and cried during one of our Zoom meetings. One of the head coaches simply said, 'Hey, listen, this is all part of the journey. You've just got to take it for what it is.' I appreciated that. I'd never had that kind of supportive and honest mentorship before. Without that direction, I would've gone in blind and made a lot of mistakes. Not that making mistakes is a bad thing – it's a good thing. But because I made the choice to find a guide, I set myself up with a blueprint, which gave me more confidence in my direction and the strategy to follow to get there.

PART THREE
WELCOME TO THE WILD

10
Warning! Danger Ahead

You're almost ready to leave captivity, to embark on your journey toward discovering what living a WILD life means to you. To do that, we first need to complete a safety check. We need to be aware of the dangers and predators we might encounter. The greatest booby traps you have to overcome are your own internal objections and the most fearsome predators are the people around you who are still living in captivity.

Beware the warnings of the pack member who has never left the safety of captivity. When you express goals and desires that vary from the norm, you're going to face a dangerous predator: the well-meaning opinions of others. People who love and care about you will, without knowing it, sabotage your success. Their well-intentioned warnings can stop your journey in its tracks, but people are so obsessed with what could go wrong that they rarely stop to consider what could go right.

Before we create your plan, we need to look at some of the most subtle and dangerous 'catch cries' of the pack that are designed to derail you and, in many cases, make the whole journey appear harder than it is. Remember that the biggest risks are associated with inaction, indecision and cowardice. The greatest predator you will face in the wild is yourself and your limited thinking. Einstein said it so well when he declared, 'We cannot solve our problems with the same thinking we used when we created them.'[58]

In the coming sections, we'll address some warning signs, red flags, potential dangers and fears about the journey ahead. Remember: you can choose not to be afraid of the dangers that you confront. The following are some common objections people have as they approach the idea of living a WILD life.

'I need to quit my job'

In our seminars and events, I often hear of people putting incredible pressure on themselves to 'burn the boats'. Their ego backs them into a corner and they feel like being successful requires that they go all-in on their vision. In many cases, 'all-in' requires sacrificing everything in their life, including what's working and making them money. There will come a

---

58   Einstein, A, *The World As I See It* (Philosophical Library, 1931)

time where you go all-in, but don't burn the boats if you can't yet see the shore.

Instead, create a transition plan. Even if you work full-time, have kids and manage to work out for an hour each day, you could arguably find twenty-plus hours a week to allocate to your side hustle, passion project or to put toward upskilling yourself for the next level of success. The truth is most people don't lack time – they lack structure and focus. You don't need more time; you need stronger focus and greater execution. In my experience, nothing sharpens the mind and focuses your energy better than a deadline. Don't be concerned by how quickly you're moving through life; be concerned by how fully you're showing up each day.

I'll always remember the moment my whole life changed. It was 22 August 2013. I had just returned home after working in Bali for six months with my then mentor, the transformational speaker Chris Howard, and was trying to start my own business. That day was a Saturday, on a weekend when I was running a two-day Business Breakthrough intensive. At the end of the session, I offered my self-mastery programme (which would go on to become my signature programme) for a cost of $1,500. Twenty people signed up on the day and became clients. In just eight hours, I had made $30,000. Considering that I had only made $16,000 for the whole of the previous year, I was blown away. In that moment I remember thinking to myself, 'I can do this.'

That is what you need to find. The moment where the stars align and you say to yourself, 'I can do this.' When that happens, feel free to burn the boats. Until that moment, be patient and keep holding on – your moment is coming.

'How will I get there?'

When you start talking about your WILD plans, people are going to doubt you. They'll want to know *how* you plan on pulling off these major life changes. In moments of doubt, many people lower their expectations and create 'how' goals when they mean to create bold goals.

Allow me to explain. A 'how' goal is one that you know how to accomplish. This makes sense in a context where we're told that we need to set SMART (specific, measurable, achievable, relevant and time-bound) goals, which emphasise being practical and realistic. While the SMART framework has merit, it assumes people know the full extent of their capabilities.[59] We've already identified that people don't fail in life because they aim high and miss but because they aim too low and hit. They could have achieved more if they set out with bold goals. You want to set goals so big that you have no idea how to reach them. There's no requirement for you to know 'how' you'll achieve

---

59 Doran, GT, 'There's a S.M.A.R.T. way to write management's goals and objectives', *Management Review*, 70 (1981), 35–36, https://community.mis.temple.edu/mis0855002fall2015/files/2015/10/S.M.A.R.T-Way-Management-Review.pdf

them, you only need to know 'who'. Ask yourself, 'Who has already achieved this goal?' Then go and ask them how they did it.

If you commit to finding a guide who can show you the way, you'll get there. At the beginning of any journey, the most important step is to craft a vision for the future that excites you. If you wait until you have mapped out every detail before you embark on the journey, you'll never get to your destination. By the time you're satisfied with your preparation, the opportunity will have passed you by. No amount of information will ever guarantee your success but taking a few important actions can have a big impact on your direction.

'It's going to be hard work'

Beware the battle cry of mediocrity that encourages you to avoid hard work. That is the voice of the masses who have relinquished their power by settling for what is easy and convenient. Your opportunity is found in the reality that creating a life of excellence is hard and takes time. The 'overnight success' story always has a backstory. What most people fail to realise is that 'hard work' and 'working hard' are different things.

Every day I wake up and work hard – but nothing I do is hard work. Yet I know plenty of people who accomplish next to nothing on any given day and complain about their life being hard. You see, all of life is hard:

- Being healthy is hard – but so is being sick
- Being rich and creating wealth is hard – so is being poor and struggling to get by
- Being committed to your life partner is hard – so is being single and alone
- Designing your best life and living it is hard – so is being stuck in a job that you hate for forty years

I say, choose your 'hard'. The antidote to a hard life isn't an easy life; it's a life of purpose where your challenges are those of your own making. Don't look for easy; look for meaningful.

'I'll do it myself'

The traditional Western school system, in so many ways, is broken. It's a system that fails too many and works for too few. One of the biggest failings of this kind of schooling is that we're conditioned to think like individuals and not tribes. In school, if someone is good at maths and I ask them for help, guidance, support and mentorship, that's called cheating. In life, that's called collaboration.

Take a moment and consider that anything you want to do in life, any field you want to go into, anything you want to create, any problem that you have in life, somebody already tackled it, studied it and has written about it. You're not going to come up with anything new, it's all out there so there's no point in reinventing the wheel. Growing up, my father used to tell me, 'There are three ways to learn in life: learn from others, learn from our own mistakes or never learn at all.' It's all about learning the success and failure of others!

This mentality is more evident in the difference between the wealthy and the rest of the world. Over the past decade, through my private coaching, I've gained a unique insight into the minds of several millionaires, multimillionaires, and billionaires and their fascinating relationship with time and money. Consistently I've seen wealthy people use their money to save and buy back their time. Whereas the clients who struggle financially often spend their time trying to save money. What many of our clients don't yet realise is that the fastest way to achieve your goals (and in the long run, the cheapest too) is to find someone who's been there, done it and to ask them how they did it.

The biggest expense in life isn't the cost of knowledge – it's the cost of ignorance. You pay for an education once and you have that knowledge forever, but you pay for ignorance over and over again. In the years before writing this book, I had stagnated in my business and income wasn't growing as it once had. I had to act, so I decided to sit down with a new mentor, someone who had grown a business to ten times the size of mine. With just one conversation, my whole mindset changed. At the time, the highest sales in any month of that year were just over $360,000. After this conversation, I revamped the business, reworked my structure and sales process, and the following week we made more than $570,000. That month we went on to break $1 million in sales. The conversation cost me about $50,000. But the cost of not having the conversation would have been $640,000. That's how much I was leaving on the table each month without the help and support of a mentor.

Beware, though, your ego will likely say one of two things at this point, either, 'We're doing well on our own, we don't need help,' or 'That's never going to work for us.' In both cases, the ego is trying to keep you safe in captivity. As author Richard Bach said, 'when you argue for your limitations you get to keep them'.[60] You're either committed to hardship and struggle or you're committed to ease, grace and speed. You'll get there eventually, but wouldn't it be more pleasant to get there together, faster and with less effort? I know what I'd prefer.

'I don't have the money to hire the best guides'

If you say that you don't have the money for advice right now, you'll never have the money. The reason for this has nothing to do with your bank account.

---

60   Bach, R, *Illusions: The adventures of a reluctant messiah* (Dell Publishing, 1977)

When you make a statement like that, you remove the option of finding, making or creating the resources you need. In my experience, doubt kills more dreams than failure ever could. When you say you don't have the money, you rob yourself of power. Successful people rarely have the resources (in this case, money) to accomplish the goals they set. Instead, they know that success is a team sport and they work to create such a compelling vision that they inspire people with money to support them.

An incredible example of this is the X Prize created by engineer, physician and entrepreneur Peter Diamandis. In 1995 Peter created the $10 million X Prize for the first team to build and launch a spacecraft capable of carrying three people to an altitude of at least 100 kilometres (62 miles) above the Earth's surface, then repeat the feat within two weeks.[61] When Peter first announced the competition, he didn't have the $10 million for the winner. Still, he moved forward with the dream, promoting the opportunity far and wide. It took eight years for someone to claim the X Prize and six years for Peter to secure the funding. If he'd waited until he had the $10 million, we might still be waiting for the X Prize winner to be announced.

Similarly, you'll be amazed by what happens when you have the courage to ask bold questions, put yourself out there and be unwavering in your commitment to the goal at hand. Mentorship doesn't have to be formal. I had dozens of informal mentors

---

61 XPRIZE Foundation, www.xprize.org/about, accessed 20 April 2023

I accessed on YouTube and through audiobooks. When you find a mentor you want to connect with, do whatever it takes to get into their proximity, learn from them and soak up their wisdom and mindset. If you can find a way to add value to their projects and endeavours, you'll be amazed at what opportunities fall onto your plate.

'I'm too busy now, I'll wait for things to get quieter'

I'm not sure about you but my life keeps getting busier, not quieter. Each year brings fresh opportunities, challenges and demands on my time, focus and energy. If something is worth doing, it's worth doing right now. I refuse to wait, settle or hesitate. I've found that not only does delay create time for other priorities to fill my calendar, but it also sets a precedent of inaction. When you choose inaction, you tell yourself and the universe that you're someone who hesitates, who isn't fully committed, who is a pushover and who flip-flops on ideas and goals. Don't wait – act now. There's never going to be a better time.

When you feel particularly time-poor, remember the Pareto principle, which states that 20% of our actions contribute to 80% of our results.[62] In essence,

---

62   De Feo, J, '80/20 Rule AKA: The Pareto Principle webinar', (Juran, 2018), www.juran.com/resources/webinars/the-pareto-principle, accessed 21 May 2022

only a few vital actions really matter. For example, if you are thinking about starting a new relationship but you never get off the couch, it's unlikely your perfect partner is going to step through the TV screen. But, if you create a dating profile and go on a date (two small actions), you increase your chance of meeting the person of your dreams and maybe going on to travel the world with them, buy a house, get married and get a cat/dog/baby/house plant. That 20% made way for the other 80%.

Here are some more ideas that will help you to take action:

- Design your goals with your time constraints in mind – use them to your advantage. If you can design your plans around travel, kids, work and studies, you have a better chance of success. Plus, when you're free of those things, you will have a massive amount of extra capacity.

- Ask yourself, 'What does my dream life look like?' If you can envision achieving your goals while you work, travel and live a WILD life, why would you hold back from your dream life in favour of your current life? Find a way to do it all.

- Wild hack: by travelling light, you can create space for more adventures. Do an audit of the activities that occupy your time and your money to determine if they are giving you fulfilment and purpose. If it's not a 'f*** yes', it's a no.

'My plan still needs work – I want it to be perfect'

Perfectionists believe they are maintaining high standards, but they're just afraid. They're afraid of being judged and their best not being good enough. Frankly, it's not. That's why we aim to always have a growth mindset. Seek progress, not perfection, and work with your tribe to create the best plan in the moment. For something to be perfected, it first needs to be created. Perfectionism is cowardice in disguise. While you're hiding and trying to make something perfect, I'm launching new products and ideas, acting on my goals, getting feedback and changing my approach. I learned a long time ago that 'done' is better than 'perfect' and not to let striving for perfection get in the way of making something better.

Apple, one of the most successful companies of all time, regularly launches products with glitches and bugs. Each time Apple launches a new phone, it's met with negative user feedback, which Apple then takes on board to create a new iOS update. Despite the bad advertising, Apple makes billions. Imagine how long we would be waiting to update our devices if Apple waited until their newest model was perfect? Imagine how much Apple would lose in revenue. I'm convinced that success is 99% determined by how quickly you can respond to failure with innovation. You get good at whatever you practise, so when you practise launching new ideas and creating momentum, you get good at that. When you hold back, you get good at hesitating.

Ask yourself what you care more about, your mission in life or what people think of you? You can't make everyone happy, so decide what is more important and then go after it. People are so busy with their own lives that they don't have time to think about your shit. Staying small and playing safe isn't serving the world.

'But what if it doesn't work?'

It's natural to want to play the 'what if' game. What if it doesn't work? What if I leave captivity and fall prey to the wild? What if it all goes wrong and I have to return home, move in with my parents and accept my status as a loser? These outcomes are all possible but they become less likely for the person who fully commits. Most people spend far more time considering what might go wrong than they do considering what could go right. The biggest mistake you can make is doing nothing. Indecision costs more than the wrong decision. At least with a mistake, you can learn, pivot and change your approach, like Apple does. With indecision, you waste time, money and the opportunity to get the feedback that is essential for success.

If you don't know where you're going, you can't make the wrong decision. Start by getting some momentum; you can always turn around and start again, but getting started is what's difficult. Then, when you have clarity on your mission, back yourself and take relentless action.

'Okay, but first I need to...'

To help you move forward, write an exhaustive list of everything you think you need to do before you begin your journey into the wild. Now, take a pen and write 'bullshit' across it. The truth is, there's nothing you need to do before you commit to living a WILD life. Just decide and act. Believe me when I say you'll be just fine. We're waiting for you.

11
Creating Your Map
Of The WILD

Congratulations, the end is near. This is perhaps the most important part of our journey together: taking the ideas, principles and concepts of this book and creating a map for you to follow. This map will show you the actions you need to take and how to implement your new knowledge effectively into your life. My experience of working with more than 200,000 people in 84 countries has allowed me to codify this map into a seven-step method that will help you become wildly successful. I call it 'The Seven Steps to WILD Success'.

Step 1: Where are you?

To create a map that will guide you through the wild, we need to know where you're starting from. If you haven't yet taken the WILD Test, go to www.wildsuccess.global/book and complete the assessment so you know exactly where you are in life right now. Start by writing down your score for each area of your life, noting what areas you need to work on to achieve your goals. By now you should be more aware of the beliefs, emotions and behaviours that contribute to the results you're seeing in these areas of your life and the actions you'll need to take to change them.

My current reality:

- Wellness

- Income

- Love

- Lifestyle

- Direction

Step 2: Where do you want to be?

What does living a WILD life mean to you? What's your definition of living life on your terms? If you need to, return to the compelling vision section of the book and consider your dream life twenty years from now. If you could have everything you desire and more, what would that look like on a day-to-day basis?

- What does that dream life look like in ten years?

- Where do you want to be in three years?

- What's different this time next year?

Step 3: Danger ahead

Every journey has risk, danger and potential road-blocks. No plan is complete without a list of potential dangers and a rough idea of how you can solve those problems when you encounter them. Consider the main dangers: not enough money, not enough time, not enough support, loss of faith, setbacks and failures.

You'll never be able to anticipate every hurdle and roadblock in your way but start with what you can see and create a plan of action and mitigation.

- Danger one:
  - My plan to mitigate, minimise and overcome:
- Danger two:
  - My plan to mitigate, minimise and overcome:
- Danger three:
  - My plan to mitigate, minimise and overcome:

Step 4: Migration duration

How long does your plan suggest it will take to get from where you are now to where you want to be? What's the timeframe for you to create and manifest your compelling vision? Most people overestimate what they can achieve in a year but underestimate what they can achieve in a decade. Each journey needs milestones along the way to allow time to stop, recharge, celebrate and restock. Break down your vision into smaller milestones along the way.

- Milestone one:

- Milestone two:

- Milestone three:

- Milestone four:

Step 5: Find your guide

The ideal guide is someone you respect, who has been where you want to go, achieved success far beyond where you are at and can help you navigate the wild. At WILD Success, we've assembled a world-leading tribe of mentors to help guide you on your journey. I have no doubt we will be able to help you find your guide in our community. It's important when you find your guide that you fully commit to their plan and don't venture off the beaten path. Often, people fail because they get distracted by the conflicting ideas and pathways to success. To find your guide, consider the following:

- What am I looking for in a guide?

- What results do I want them to have achieved?

- How do I want to be supported by my guide?

- Is there anything specific I need help and support with on my journey?

Step 6: Find your tribe

Show me your friends and I'll show you who you are. It's often said that you're the sum of the five people you associate with the most. Ask yourself:

- Who believes in me?

- Who's more successful than me?

- Who's living a WILD life?

- Who's got my back?

- Who's heading on the same journey as me?

- Who leaves me feeling inspired and energised?

If you have a long list, congratulations. If you don't, then it's time to upgrade your inner circle. I've found that the best way to attract my tribe is to put myself in growth environments by attending seminars, mastermind groups or think tanks. People who are open to growth seek out and support people who are on the same path.

Write the name of your five closest friends, allies and support team who are on the journey with you.

Only write the names of people who meet the criteria above and leave any spaces blank for new people who are yet to join your tribe.

1.

2.

3.

4.

5.

Step 7: Bold actions

The final step is to write a list of bold actions that you can take right now to implement the lessons you have learned from this book.

Commit *right now* by writing a list of actions that will launch your adventure in search of a WILD life.

You didn't come this far to stop now. Take the next step into the wild. Follow your map to help you define what you've been put on this planet to do.

This is your moment.

Interview: Kim Barrett

A success story that I'm particularly proud of is that of my dear friend, mentor and business partner, Kim Barrett. Kim was one of only eleven people at my first seminar (eight of the other audience members were my relatives). After that first one, he attended all of my events until we eventually started working together. He was instrumental in helping me make my first million and, more importantly, helping our message reach every corner of the globe. Kim used what he'd learned through WILD Success to start one of Australia's leading social media agencies www.yoursocialvoice.com.au. He's a self-made millionaire who has created an incredible company and life that allows him the freedom to travel the world.

What makes this story even more extraordinary is that, three years after I met Kim, he introduced me to someone who would change my life forever. On 20 February 2019, surrounded by our friends and family, I took Ashlee Barrett, Kim's sister, to be my wife and partner in life. The ceremony was officiated by none other than Kim himself. I don't know what made Kim come along to that first event – maybe I should ask him one day – but I do know that I wouldn't be here today without him. The universe has plans for us that we know nothing about. In this interview, we talk about the WILD lives we've created together.

Calvin: What does 'living a WILD life' mean to you?

Kim: Living a WILD life means that you're living the life of your choosing, free from anyone else dictating how you should be living. A WILD life is one where you can get out there, you can do, be and achieve whatever you set your mind to.

Calvin: How important is unshakeable self-belief in living a WILD life?

Kim: Self-belief is what makes you strive forward. If I didn't have self-belief, none of the businesses that I have built, the outcomes that I've been able to achieve or the adventures I've had would be possible. Without unshakeable self-belief, you can't achieve beyond your dreams. You must first believe that you can achieve whatever you set your mind to; then, having self-belief will grant you the power of knowing that what you focus on is what you can do.

Calvin: Can you tell us about how overcoming a limiting belief helped you to achieve success? And were you able to identify where that limiting belief came from?

Kim: My limiting beliefs go way back, as in past-life regression. When I analysed the limiting beliefs around my self-confidence, I had a feeling that they didn't come from anything that had happened to me, not even anything I'd experienced growing up in my family environment. Luckily, utilising the techniques that I learned as part of my WILD Success experience, I was able to access and identify some of those limiting beliefs and overcome them. A major hurdle for me, which I think a lot of people go through, is thinking: who am I to speak and teach people? Who am I to think people want to listen to me? That inner critic saying, 'I'm not good enough, not smart enough, not the right person.'

A key factor that contributed to my success was the ability to identify that lack of self-belief, to identify when I was putting myself down, and being able to release myself from that captivity. Without doing that first, I would have been unable to move forward. For example, overcoming the limiting belief of, 'Who am I to be doing this?' allowed me to step up in front of a digital stage of over 50,000 people. I've spoken on stages all around the world and every time I do something like that the self-doubt creeps in but, with my unshakeable self-belief in place, it's easy to step past the doubt and shoot for the stars.

Calvin: What advice do you have for someone to help them go beyond aiming for what they think they can achieve to aiming for what they truly desire from life?

Kim: My advice is this: every single thing that you want to do and achieve, unless you're Elon Musk putting people on Mars, has already been done. Steve Jobs is reported to have said, 'Anything that you see, anything that you do, has been created by people who are no smarter than you.' Whatever you want from life, whether that's sitting on a beach sipping coconuts and earning a passive income, or being able to help people remove their own self-doubt, or being with the person you want to be with, it has already been achieved by someone else. You need to remove any impact barriers you think would hold you back from success. Remove the fear, the shame and the vulnerability, because not only have all the achievements already been achieved, so too have all the failures. Edison supposedly said, 'I didn't fail 10,000 times creating the lightbulb. I came up with 10,000 ways that didn't work.' That is the mindset to have. You're not failing, you've just figured out all the things that haven't worked so far, which means you're on track to finding what *is* going to work. So why not shoot for the stars, right? Why not go for what you truly desire to have in your life? Why not? There's literally no answer to that.

Calvin: Talk to me about the importance of emotional mastery.

Kim: Being able to master your emotions, to understand and identify specifically what you're feeling during any interaction or event, is what takes someone from good to great. Especially if you're someone who wants to start a business, or if you're coaching and working with clients, or anything along those lines, you're going to experience, and be required to manage, a rollercoaster of emotions.

Emotions are constant and, when you're building a business or working with clients, you deal with both your own emotions and those of the people you work with. From the moment you wake up, you're going to face fires you need to put out. From the moment you wake up, you're going to have hurdles and obstacles you need to solve and overcome. That is the reality you will need to learn to navigate. Living a WILD life with emotional mastery means having the foresight to navigate that terrain. It's being able to ride that emotional rollercoaster and not throw up at the end of it.

Calvin: What have you done to master your emotions and what suggestions do you have for someone trying to improve how they react or process their emotions?

Kim: I think being able to pause, to feel the emotions and be aware of what is going on is hugely powerful in terms of being able to react in a calm, cool manner. Recently, I've experienced some staff changes in my business. I've been onboarding new people and farewelling people I thought were going to be with me for a long time. When I had exit meetings with them, which had the potential to be emotionally charged, I chose not to react negatively or positively during those interactions. I was able to communicate with them and process what was going on without losing myself to the emotion.

This is all about awareness. The first port of call is being able to identify when something triggers an extreme level of positivity or an extreme level of negativity, which is going to drive you to one reaction or another. Many people try and shoot for happiness and positivity all the time, but I would ask instead, 'How do I make sure that my average setting is neutral?' because from there, it's much easier to adjust your reaction. If you experience super-high highs or super-low lows, you're going to get a bouncing effect. This is detrimental because if you are always shifting you will never experience neutral. The result is that you're more easily set off. If you can find neutrality, then when you experience something amazing or heartbreaking, you are able to feel it and navigate that emotion more consciously.

Calvin: What rituals and behaviours have helped you create success in life?

Kim: The commitment to creating powerful behaviours is a major component of living my WILD life. My behaviours provide the structure I need to be primed for success because that success relies on consistency. Whichever primary behaviour you practise will have the greatest impact on your life. Identifying my bad habits and replacing them with powerful behaviours has helped me to achieve my current level of success.

Getting up early and going to the gym is my primary behaviour. Doing my workout first thing in the morning lets me start the day with a positive mindset. Going to the gym and doing an intense workout will be the most difficult thing my body is going to feel all day, right? Anything that happens after that is easy. Implementing that powerful behaviour replaced my previous bad habit of waking up and going straight for coffee and bad food, which resulted in me coasting through the day and having no energy at the end of it. I have an addictive personality, which means if I start something, I don't stop until it becomes a habit, until it becomes a behaviour, until it becomes a new addiction.

Calvin: What is your recommendation for someone trying to implement powerful behaviours?

Kim: The key is to condition yourself to take the first step. Identifying the first positive step in the sequence is important because it will have a domino effect on every decision that follows. For example, it's much harder for me to eat terrible food after I've done a workout in the morning. I've done the workout and I feel good about myself, so I'm much less likely to go through a drive-through for a burger, six hash browns and extra cheesy fries.

The other big piece is accountability. I have my trainer from the gym and a peak performance coach who both hold me accountable by monitoring my stats. I track everything, bringing visibility to my results, which is the final piece. Seeing or quantifying the results of your powerful behaviour will motivate you to do more of the same.

Calvin: Why do you believe that having a single point of focus and not letting life distract you is so important to long-term success?

Kim: There's a saying that the man who chases several rabbits catches none. You want to have one core focus, one core outcome that you're working toward at any time. There have been several times where I would be working, I would be trying to run a side hustle and I'd be looking for new opportunities, but it wouldn't work or my results would be poor. On the flip side, when I focus on one key objective at a time, I know I can move progressively toward that goal and I can achieve it.

Calvin: Why is it so important to have a proven strategy, as opposed to making it up as you go?

Kim: I mentioned previously that anything we want to do has already been done by someone else, so why try and reinvent the wheel? If there is a step-by-step method for you to follow, why wouldn't you use it? That WILD life that you want to live? Someone is already living it, or something close to it, so why would you not follow that same strategy to achieve your goals more efficiently and effectively?

Calvin: How do you know when it's time to change your approach and adopt a new strategy?

Kim: It's when the results don't show. Not getting the results that you want is a pretty big indicator that your strategy's not working. Of course, you need to identify the problem. Is it strategy? Awesome. Then you can change it. You can try a different way, just make sure you know why you're changing course and the outcome you want to achieve by doing that.

If you're on a path and it's not working, the first thing I would recommend is that you reassess if you're on the right path. Second, do you have all the skills required to travel that path? Do you know how to walk? Because you need that skill before you can run, skip or fly. Once you are sure you have the skills, you can follow a proven strategy from someone who's been there and you are likely to achieve success by doing exactly that.

Calvin: With each of those topics in mind, how has finding a mentor impacted your journey?

Kim: Mentorship has impacted my journey through the accelerating effect my mentors have had on my success. You can still get where you're going without a mentor but you're going to make more mistakes, encounter more hurdles to jump over and you're going to face the challenges alone. With a mentor, you have the benefit of leaning on the experience of someone who has already done it, has already walked that path and already achieved your goal. Why *wouldn't* you get a mentor to help you?

Finding a mentor helped me acquire the tools to identify and manage my emotions. Getting help with that meant that it became easier for me to have conversations with people. My mentor taught me the framework of listening with the intent to understand versus the intent to respond through active listening. When I switched from passively letting the messages and intentions of others pass over me and really started understanding what they were saying, why they were saying it and how their viewpoint could differ from mine, my communication and how I reacted in response to others changed entirely.

Finding a mentor helped me hone my focus. I had a guide to encourage and push me to focus on one key thing, which was starting my business and taking a deep dive into marketing.

Finding a mentor helped me understand my direction and gave me the confidence to follow it by providing an example of a proven strategy. I was able to take a step back and consider, 'Am I following in the footsteps of someone who's done the same thing? Or am I walking while following a runner? Am I running while following a flyer? Am I flying while following a skipper?' Once I figured out the right path to follow, I could then find the mentor who had done that and say to myself, 'Yeah, cool. This is how to step. This is how to break-dance. This is how to fly. This is how you do whatever it is that you want to do.'

Conclusion

The perspective shifts, methodology and advice presented in this book are a culmination of years of work. Neither the case study participants nor I arrived at the WILD life easily or by chance, so don't make comparisons or feel defeated about where you are in your life. You are precisely where you need to be and you are in a position of great power. You have assessed the landscape around you and can work toward establishing or clarifying your vision. You are prepared to challenge your beliefs, assess your emotions and evaluate your habits and focus. You are armed with the knowledge that while stepping out in a new direction will bring new challenges, you can reach for a helping hand from someone with the precise wisdom you need to find your feet. You are ready to discover what living a WILD life means to you.

A WILD invitation

The fact that you're reading these words places you in a rare group of committed people. I know there's a fire inside of you that's calling you to achieve more. While I don't know what made you pick up this book, I do believe there's a higher force guiding our actions and movements. We are kindred spirits on this journey into the wild together.

To that end, I want to meet you. I want to support you on your journey. I want you to join me in the wild where you belong. Your time is now. Despite the upheaval of global events in recent years, this is the best time in human history to be alive. Together, we will achieve wonders.

My final words of wisdom as you begin this sacred journey towards WILD Success are these: in every great story, there is a moment when you think the hero is about to fail. You are that hero and your commitment will be tested. If this was easy, everyone would do it. I urge you to endure and keep to the path. Know that throughout your journey you will venture off-path many times. That's to be expected. Enjoy the wilderness – the views along the way are quite magnificent. Then, take time to check the map and get yourself back on track. You have a duty to forge tracks for others who, like you, will find the courage to venture beyond the gates of captivity. Your success, like mine, will not be measured by what you achieve but by what you help others achieve.

They say the best way for a person to die is at an old age, lying peacefully in a warm bed, surrounded by loved ones and filled with proud memories of a life well lived. Yet too many people die too young, surrounded by angry and confused faces. They're the faces of books never written, dreams never pursued, businesses never created, first kisses never had, love never nurtured, songs never sung and a destiny never fulfilled. In your final moments, these missed opportunities look at you and say, 'We came to you, for only you could have given us life and now we must die with you.' If you were to leave this life too soon, what books, ideas, songs, businesses, loves and legacies would die with you?

There's never been a better time to be exceptional; you live in a world full of magic and wonder. Anything is possible if you have the courage to succeed, try, fail and get back up again.

Now that you're ready to move forward, take the WILD oath. Raise your right hand and repeat, out loud, the following:

'I fully commit to living a WILD life. I commit to freeing myself and those I love from a life of captivity so that together we may live life on our terms. I begin my journey into the WILD and follow the road less travelled because it calls to my heart and soul. I want to live a life of true freedom and will accept nothing less than the fullest expression of a life well lived.

The road ahead is long and hard but I know it will be worth it. It will take everything I've got but I have what it takes. I refuse to settle for anything less in my life than what I truly desire. I refuse to accept the status quo. I reject mediocrity and am fully committed to living my WILDest dreams. I will use my gifts and talents to make this world a better place and I will share my wisdom with those I love. I have taken my first step into the WILD and now there is no looking back.

I am WILD.'

Here's to your journey ahead. Be bold. Have fun. Make an impact. Welcome to the WILD.

Calvin Coyles

Connect with WILD Success

You've reached the end and might be left with the distinct feeling that, while you may have finished the book, your part of the story is only just beginning.

Here are the ways to get in touch and learn how the WILD team and I can help you accelerate towards your WILD life:

- 🌐 https://wildsuccess.global
- ⓕ www.facebook.com/calvincoylesofficial
- ⓘ @CalvinCoyles
- ▶ www.youtube.com/user/calvincoyles
- ✉ support@wildsuccess.global

Or just swing by to say hello. We'd love to follow your journey.

Acknowledgements

Until you write a book yourself, you don't fully appreciate the acknowledgement sections of other books, filled with the names of people who have supported the author in their journey. In this case, the adage of 'it takes a village' certainly applies. There are simply too many people to list here, but I will endeavour to celebrate a few who have helped beyond measure.

To my editor, Debby Vinciullo: if you knew the full extent of what this project involved when you came on board, you probably would have said no. You have been so much more than an editor; your name should replace mine on the cover, because you took the ramblings of a dyslexic motivational speaker and made them into an incredible book. Thank you for being my co-pilot on the journey, I can't wait for our next adventure.

To Daniel Priestley, your wisdom and counsel have shaped this book into what it is today – thank you for your belief and guidance.

To the whole team at Rethink Press – Lucy McCarraher, Ysabel Legaspi, Jennifer Scott, Anke Ueberberg, Sarah Marchant, Abi Willford and Katrina Lobley. You have been unbelievably patient with me and worked tirelessly to make this book the best it can be. Thank you.

To Chris Howard, your mentorship is the foundation upon which this book was built. I am forever your student and will always be in your debt.

To TJ and Liv Jones, ever since that coffee in St Ali's I've been trying to keep up with the Joneses. Your mentorship and impact on my life has been immeasurable.

To Brett and Marie Jones, thank you for giving your time to a young man with unjustified self-confidence. You are the embodiment of a true partnership in every sense of the word.

To Roy McDonald, thank you for asking me what I was going to do with the rest of my life and for the abundance you have shared with my family. Karen Hyslop, I have no words for the example you have set. You, perhaps more than anyone, need not read this book, for you are already living it.

To Hanalei Swan, Andrew Pearce, Casey O Anaru, Elsa Morgan, Travis Jones, Kim Barrett and Karim El Barche, thank you for the contributions you have made to the book with your vulnerability and wisdom.

To the whole team at WILD Success, you are rockstars and have made this last decade a life-changing adventure.

To Kim, what a decade we've had. I could ask for no better friend and partner. Jason, together we've made magic happen for people all over the world – thank you for all that you have done, you are truly a warrior of light. Karim and Simon, your friendship means more than you know.

To my brothers and sister, I am unbelievably proud of you. I strive to be an example for you all. To CJ, never stop being unapologetically yourself, the world is better for it.

To Ron and Bernadette, thank you for betting on yourselves when no one else did. Elizabeth and James Brian, you've instilled into me the belief in spirit and in myself that has filled these pages. I'd be lost without you.

To Mum, who I love more than anything, thank you for teaching me unconditional love. Dad, at least 90% of the quotes in this book I stole from you. I hope to share your wisdom, guidance and strength with the world.

To my wife, Ashlee, you're the best thing to ever happen to me. Your love is the wind that fills our sails. Alila Rae, what a blessing you are. I wrote this book for you. I hope you take these pages and make their lessons your own.

To all the people who have attended our seminars, workshops and retreats over the past ten years, thank you for the opportunity to share my gifts with you and to share in your life. The lessons I have learned with you fill these pages and my heart. I am forever your humble servant.

The Author

Calvin Coyles arrived in Australia in 1994 after emigrating with his family from the mining town of Sunderland, United Kingdom. At twelve he was selected out of hundreds to receive a specialist drama scholarship at the prestigious John Curtin College of the Arts where he would spend five years learning theatre and performance.

After graduating, he studied law and commerce at the University of Western Australia where he was awarded the designation of International Excellence Ambassador in 2010 for his work in Africa leading micro finance projects. He led Australia to the semifinals of the World Cup for Social Enterprise (SIFE) in 2011 and in 2012 built his own nonprofit company with more than 150 volunteer staff.

In 2013, Calvin left Australia and spent the next year working for free-learning NLP, Mindset, Motivation & Personal Development. Arriving back in Australia in more than $40,000 of debt, Calvin started his own business and grew it to $1,000,000 in revenue in ten months. Since then, he's never looked back.

After nearly a decade working in personal transformation, NLP and breakthrough coaching, he is now the CEO of his own company, WILD Success. From his experience supporting 200,000 clients in over eighty countries, he developed the WILD Method, a breakthrough way of producing transformational change for people. He's led training programmes for leaders, coaches, healers, athletes and business owners in over fifty countries.

At just thirty-three, Calvin is a self-made multimillionaire, has published three best-selling books and has been featured alongside Tony Robbins, Deepak Chopra and Jeff Bezos in publications including *Forbes, Entrepreneur Magazine, Huffington Post, INC* and *Business Insider,* and was named as one of the top ten conscious male thought leaders to watch in 2022 by *USA Today.*

He is a husband, father, business owner, angel investor and philanthropist. He lives in Perth, Western Australia with his family.

www.ingramcontent.com/pod-product-compliance
Lightning Source LLC
Chambersburg PA
CBHW070030100426

42740CB00013B/2648